MIND · BODY · SPIRIT

I AM AWESOME

A Healthy Workbook for Kids

MARY RICHARDS

FSP
FIRST STEPS PUBLISHING

I AM AWESOME! *A Healthy Workbook for Kids*
by Mary Richards

© 2014 by Mary Richards. All rights reserved.
AwesomeWorkbook.com

First Print Edition, August 2014

Limit of Liability / Disclaimer Warranty

The publisher and the author make no representation or warranties with respect to the accuracy or completeness of the contents of this work. This work is sold with the understanding that the publisher is not engaged in rendering mental health evaluations or other professional services. Neither the author nor the publisher shall be liable for damages arising utilizing this work or any website cited as a potential source of further information.

At the time of this book's publication, all facts and figures cited are the most current available; phone numbers, addresses and Web site URLs are accurate and active; all publications, organizations, Web sites and other resources exist as described in this book and have been verified. The author and First Steps Publishing make no warranty or guarantee concerning the information and materials given out by organizations, or content found at Web sites, and are not responsible for any changes that occur after this books' publication. If you find an error or believe that a resource listed here is not as described, please contact First Steps Publishing.

Permission is granted for individual readers, parents, teachers and group leaders to photocopy pages for personal, home, classroom or group work only. Photocopying or other reproduction of these materials for an entire school or school system is strictly forbidden.

The opinions expressed by the author are not necessarily those of First Steps Publishing.

Published by First Steps Publishing
105 Westwind Street | Box 571 | Gleneden Beach, Oregon 97388
www.FirstStepsPublishing.com

© 2014 by Mary Richards. All Rights reserved.
Cover illustration/ Interior illustrations by Carrie Brand, Carrieliarts.com
Interior graphics provided by Shutterstock.com
Cover design / Interior layout and design by Suzanne Fyhrie Parrott

---

Published in the United States of America

Library of Congress Control Number 2014912787

Richards, Mary

    I am Awesome! A Healthy Workbook for Kids
    p.cm.
    Includes bibliographical references

    ISBN13 978-1-937333-06-5
    ISBN10 1937333065

    1. Juvenile Nonfiction—Activity Books. 2. Juvenile Nonfiction—Social Issues—Self-Esteem & Self-Reliance.
    3. Juvenile Nonfiction—Social Issues—Friendship. 4. Juvenile Nonfiction—Health & Daily Living—Maturing.
    5. Juvenile Nonfiction—Health & Daily Living—Fitness & Exercise. 6. Adolescence. 7. Emotional Maturity. I. Title

08.01.14

Please provide feedback.
PRINTED IN THE U.S.A.

WHAT THEY'RE SAYING...

I Am Awesome! A Healthy Workbook for Kids is a wholesome and well-rounded introduction to the six areas of maturity which the author, Mary Richards, has chosen to include in her book. It gives the owner an organized opportunity to research many areas of interest or need, or something they've never thought about before. I can see where it could be an excellent tool in a counseling situation, where the young person can be aided in setting personal goals for growth or possible healing. Although this workbook would not replace a health curriculum, it could be a supplementary project for tweens and young teen students, both boys and girls. And, even though not Christian related in its overall verbiage, it is open-ended enough that any young person can make this book their own by what they choose to write.

—Colleen Busch, 25 years of homeschooling experience

As an educator and child and family therapist I am exceptionally pleased to know that *I Am Awesome* is being offered as a resource for our youth and their families. Through years of teaching and working through these activities with her students, Ms. Richards has compiled page after page of pertinent health and wellness concepts and activities. Plus, her dynamic and engaging teaching style comes through in her writing as she talks directly to her readers. *I Am Awesome* is a health and wellness activity workbook that can be used not only by an individual, but also with parent interaction/guidance. I also see it as a wonderful resource for educators and facilitators working with youth and groups in a multitude of different settings.

—Carolynn R. Hamilton, Ph.D. Psychologist

This book is not only awesome; this is it! Finally we have an effective and enduring resource for in and out of school use. As a life science researcher and educator with a wealth of experience in grades kindergarten through college, I have reviewed abundant health education curricula. Many also purport to "build character," but they all end up gathering dust on the shelf. This workbook will engage and guide youth in a comprehensive search for identity. While directing her attention to middle school kids, Ms. Richards speaks to all who aspire to lifelong growth and development.

—Jacqueline B. Rojas, Ph.D. Science Education

I like how I can make lists and fill in the pages and come back to it later. I think the breaking bad habits section will help me a lot. This book asks a lot of good questions. This book is awesome! I want to start filling it out now!

—Logan, age 10, grade 5

As a teacher, we're told about how important it is to show that our students are learning. This book truly educates the whole child. As a parent, this book helps guide me in all parts of my child's growth, and provides tools for us to be successful.

—Joe, Middle School Language Arts/ Social Studies teacher, and Logan's parent

My favorite subjects in the book are: *My Relationships,* because it reminded me of where I came from, who loves me, and who surrounds me; *Inspirational Thoughts for (My) Personal Maturity*--I love how it makes me look into myself, and evaluate my actions; *My Skills and Talents*—This shows me what I have in my knowledge and how I can teach others.

—Jorja, age 11, grade 6

I love the book because it focuses on children's personal achievements and goals, and has them look into themselves as individuals. It also teaches kids life lessons, not academic lessons, but at the same time helps them focus on how to achieve academically! Also, this book helps educate kids about who they are...and how they learn as a person and grow! Great Book!!

—Cindy, Dental Hygienist, and parent of Jorja

As a social worker I work with at-risk families daily. Educating and providing parents with tools is very important in not only helping with attachment to their children, but also breaking generational cycles of unhealthy behaviors (i.e. abuse, neglect) within the family dynamic. *I Am Awesome* takes a holistic approach in helping our youth and gives us yet another tool as parents, educators, and society in general, in helping to raise & protect the most precious things to us, our children. I am excited to not only use it with my own children but with the families/parents I work with. What a user-friendly and great resource this workbook truly is!

—Shelly Barr, QMHA

THIS BOOK BELONGS TO:

_____

Age: _____

Birth date: _____

Today's date: _____

Grade in school: _____

 **INTRODUCTION**

INTRODUCTION

If you are someone who would like to celebrate how unique and wonderful you already are, and explore ways of developing yourself into an even more awesome individual, then this book is for you. I have always had a passion for helping kids recognize their uniqueness and the control they can have while developing into a well-balanced and happy individual. That's why, in this book, I am addressing all of the ways in which one can mature: personally, emotionally, physically, socially, intellectually and ethically. These six areas are explained in more detail on the following page.

I Am Awesome is organized into chapters that address each of the areas of maturity, with an appendix that provides helpful information and resources. The activities in this book could be shared with a friend or relative, or kept private. Be sure to communicate with your loved ones about whether or not they can peek in your book, or if they need permission to take a look.

Hopefully you will enjoy this book and find the information helpful and interesting. It should be fun to look back at your thoughts and ideas as you go through life. If this book helps boost at least one person's self esteem, then it will have been worth the time and effort.

– Mary Richards

INTRODUCTION

THE SIX AREAS OF MATURITY

Some people think of maturity as just the changes that take place in your body physically, as you go through puberty, but there are actually six different ways we mature as human beings:

- **Personally**—gaining self-knowledge and self esteem by trying to work on feeling better about ourselves and our potential.

- **Emotionally**--being aware of and able to understand and control our feelings and thoughts; developing a positive outlook on life.

- **Physically**—taking good care of ourselves as our bodies grow and develop, especially in terms of a healthy diet, adequate exercise, getting enough sleep, and staying safe.

- **Socially**—making and keeping friends; improving our communication skills; being at ease with a variety of people.

- **Intellectually**--understanding the importance of learning about the world around us; gaining knowledge about our interests; expanding our creative minds.

- **Ethically**--developing a sense of right and wrong; deciding how we want to be perceived; becoming a responsible citizen.

This book will focus on each of these areas of maturity, with activities that will help you be more aware of how you are developing and maturing as an individual. Maturation is a lifelong process. Everyone can benefit from continuing to learn about themselves, and trying to develop further in all areas of maturity.

TABLE OF CONTENTS

CHAPTER 1 - PERSONAL MATURITY:

About Personal Maturity—2; All About Me—3; My Favorite People and Things—4-7; Lyrics to My Favorite Songs—8-9; Favorite Books and Movies—10; Book and Movie Recommendations—11; How I See Myself—12; My Skills and Talents—13; My Relationships—14; My Support System—15; Holidays, Anniversaries and Birthdays—16; Adult Interview—17; My Personal Acrostic—18; Compliments—19-21; What am I Going to Do When I Grow Up?—22; My Bucket List—23; My Achievements So Far—24 My Timeline—25; Inspirational Thoughts For Personal Maturity—26-27; Personal Goals – 28-29.

CHAPTER 2 - EMOTIONAL MATURITY:

About Emotional Maturity—32; Simple Pleasures—33-34; Visualizing My Own Special Place—35-36; My Dreams—37; Blast Away Boredom—38; Affirmations—39-42; My Privacy Sign—43; Problem-Solving Practice—44; 21 Days to Success!—45-46; My Pushbuttons—47; Stress Busters—48-49; Relaxation Tips to Try—50; Grieving Through Losses in Life—51-53; Turning Around Negative Self-Talk—54; Celebrating the Good Choices I have Made in My Life—55; Journaling—56-58; Inspirational Thoughts for Emotional Maturity—59-60; Emotional Goals—61-62,

CHAPTER 3 - PHYSICAL MATURITY:

About Physical Maturity—64; Important Numbers in Case of an Emergency—65; Safety Survey—66; Am I Getting Enough Sleep?—67; How Good is My Hygiene?—68; Do I Take Good Care of My Vertebrae?—69; Am I a Nutrition Wizard?—70-72; How Good Are My Eating Habits?—73; Healthy Snacks—74-75; What Dietary Changes Am I Willing to Make?—76; My Food Log—77; Which Sports and Activities Sound Interesting?—78; Researching Local Sports and Activities—79; My Pedometer Log—80-81; Physical Challenges—82-84; Physical Activities I Can Do Alone and With Others—85; Inspirational Thoughts for Physical Maturity—86-87; Physical Goals—88-89.

CHAPTER 4 - SOCIAL MATURITY:

About Social Maturity—92; My Neighborhood—93; Local Activities to Do With Family and Friends—94; Get People Talking!—95-96; How Good Are My Manners—97-98; Smile Experiment—99; Ad for a Friend—100; What We Have in Common, and What Makes Us Unique—101; Refusal Skills—102-103; Am I a Good Listener?—104; Coupons—105; How to Make Friends—106; Inspirational Thoughts for Social Maturity—107-108; Social Goals—109-110.

CHAPTER 5 - INTELLECTUAL MATURITY:

About Intellectual Maturity—112; What Genre of Book Interests Me the Most?—113; Expanding My Horizons—114; Time to Work on Study Skills—115; Successful Study Skills—116-117; School Supplies Checklist—118; Classmates to Call for Help With Homework Questions—119; Help! A Project!—120; Study and Activity Planner—121; Example of a Page From an Agenda Notebook—122; What Are My Strongest Areas of Intelligence?—123-124; Ways to Improve and Enjoy Each Area of Intelligence—125-127; Mock Job Interview—128-129; Do I Want to Raise Some Dough?—130; Sample Flyer or Business Card—131; Fun With Cartooning!—132-133; Having Fun With Idioms—134-136; Designing My Own T-Shirt—137-138; Plan A Party!—139; Inspirational Thoughts For Intellectual Maturity—140-141; Intellectual Goals—142-143.

CHAPTER 6 - ETHICAL MATURITY:

About Ethical Maturity—146; Volunteering to Help Others—147-149; My Opinions—150; What Are My Values?—151; Thinking Ahead About Consequences—152; Empathy—153-154; Empathy Challenges—155; What Would I Like My Epitaph to Say?—156; When Was the Last Time I Did a RAK? (Random Act of Kindness)—157; My 'RAK' Log—158; Who Are My Role Models?—159; Inspirational Thoughts For Ethical Maturity—160-161; Ethical Goals—162-163.

APPENDIX -

Birth Signs—166; Fun and Interesting Days to Celebrate Each Year—167; Things to Do When You're Bored at Home:—170; Party Theme Ideas—173; Easy to Make or Find: Stress Relievers—174; Play Dough Recipe—175; Skills You Can Teach Yourself—176; What Does A Serving Size Look Like?—177; 8 Ways to Say "No" to Peer Pressure—178; Things to Think About When Setting Goals—179; Things to Think About When Dealing With Loss—180; Signs and Symptoms That You or a Friend Might Have an Eating Disorder—181; Helplines—182; Decision-making Help: HALTS!—183; Types of College Degrees—184.

BIBLIOGRAPHY—185-187

CHAPTER 1

PERSONAL MATURITY

CHAPTER 1 ~ PERSONAL MATURITY

ABOUT PERSONAL MATURITY

Did you know that you are awesome? Think about it. No one but you has your DNA, your fingerprints, your smile, your thoughts or your experiences. Pretty unique, huh? It's up to you to believe in yourself and make the most of the opportunities that are out there for you.

This first chapter concentrates on celebrating who you are, and who has helped you along the way. When you work on personal maturity you're working on your self-concept, or how you see yourself, both inside and out. It's important to learn as much as you can about yourself, so you can have more confidence in your ability to go out in the world and reach your goals.

Remember, you are already awesome. Now it's time to celebrate how wonderful and unique you are, and to work on self-improvement, so you can become a happier, more well-rounded person.

CHAPTER 1 ~ PERSONAL MATURITY

ALL ABOUT ME!

Fill in the blanks below as best as you can. The Internet can be a wonderful source for what specific names mean, what your birth sign is, and, what your birth sign might say about what kind of person you are. Some people might say that you should "take the information with a grain of salt", but it's still fun to look into.

My full name is: _____ .

My first name, _____, means _____ .

My middle name, _____, means _____ .

My last name, _____, means _____ .

I was born on the _____ day of _____ in the year _____ .
                                   month

My birth sign* is _____. This means that perhaps I possess these qualities: _____ .

I was born in the Chinese year of the ** _____ .

So, I might have these qualities: _____ .

I weighed _____ pounds and _____ ounces when I was born, and the approximate time of day was _____. My relatives tell me that my ancestors came from these countries: _____

_____

_____ .

*Learn what your birth sign is on page 166 in the Appendix.

** Look up the Chinese calendar on the Internet. It will tell you what animal sign you were born under, and what qualities might be characteristic of that sign.

 **CHAPTER 1 ~ PERSONAL MATURITY**

MY FAVORITE PEOPLE AND THINGS!

Part of what can make you feel unique in the world is when you begin to develop an interest in the places and people around you. No two people, not even identical twins, have the same thoughts and feelings. You can develop special interests that might be different from your siblings and friends. You can also choose who you want to form close relationships with, sometimes even to the extent of choosing a special pet that is all your own, (and your own responsibility, don't forget!).

It's fun to take an interest in something and try to learn more about it. Becoming good at something, and knowing more about the world around you, your likes and dislikes, helps you mature personally. It also will help you feel better about yourself, and more confident and happy in your everyday life. Try not to become too focused, however, on just one thing. Have you ever heard the phrase, "Variety is the spice of life"? It's best to be well-rounded in your knowledge and experiences, so that you can fit in with the variety of people you will need to communicate with throughout your life, in school, on the job, and just out in the world.

Fill in the next few pages with your favorites, and then keep in mind other topics you can add on the page that has blank categories. These "favorites" will perhaps change over the years, but that's all part of exploring your choices and figuring out just what you are all about.

CHAPTER 1 ~ PERSONAL MATURITY

MY FAVORITE...

Thing to Do

Movie

TV Show

Actor/Actress

Cartoon Character

Sport to Play

Teacher

Subject

Animal

Book

F o o d

Sport to Watch

Qualitiy I Like About Myself

Food to Prepare

Hobby

Quote:

CHAPTER 1 ~ PERSONAL MATURITY

MORE OF MY FAVORITES...

Summer Memory

Musical Artist or Group

Place to Hang Out

Quality About My Parent(s) or Guardian(s):

Type of Food

School Memory

Same Sex Friend

Opposite Sex Friend

Computer Game

Type of Car

Family Activity

CHAPTER 1 ~ PERSONAL MATURITY

CREATING MY OWN FAVORITES

Add your own topics in the boxes below.

CHAPTER 1 ~ PERSONAL MATURITY

 # LYRICS!
TO ONE OF MY
FAVORITE SONGS

Look up the words to one of your favorite songs, and write or paste them into the space below. Or, write your own song (or poem) on this page. Don't forget to write down the title, composer/singer, and the year it was written.

CHAPTER 1 ~ PERSONAL MATURITY

TO SOME OF MY

MY FAVORITE BOOKS & MOVIES

Here's a good place to keep track of your favorite books and movies over the years.

CHAPTER 1 ~ PERSONAL MATURITY

BOOK & MOVIE RECOMMENDATIONS

Ask friends and relatives which books and movies they've enjoyed. Research websites.

BOOKS	MOVIES

HOW I SEE MYSELF

There are many ways to describe a person. Below is a list of descriptive words and phrases. Some are desirable, some are not so desirable. Circle the ones that you feel describe you. If there are some qualities you wish you could circle, put a star by those qualities and then try to improve on those traits. Be proud of yourself for all of the positive qualities you've circled. You may need to look up some of the words, or ask someone for help with understanding. Are there some undesirable qualities you circled that you need to work on? We all possess qualities to be proud of, and probably some that we need to work on, in an effort to be more personally mature.

eager   cool   grumpy   relaxed   coordinated   serious
mathematical   proud   arrogant   open-minded   courageous
moody   hyper   creative   well-adjusted   smart   shy
good communicator   explosive   approachable   calm   bored
adventurous   messy   resilient   sweet   athletic   loud
stubborn   friendly   patient   motivated   argumentative
attractive   competitive   gutsy   musical   difficult   strong
giving   loyal   decisive   agreeable   egotistical   anxious
fair   appreciative   enthusiastic   modest   fun   forgiving
likable   impatient   happy   funny   talented   compassionate
good pet owner   good listener   lucky   awkward
leader   confident   aimless   sarcastic
dancer   honest   careful   pleasant
spiritual   caring   achiever   artist   fit
intriguing   expressive   negative   optimistic
spontaneous   jealous   mischievous

MY SKILLS AND TALENTS

You probably have a lot of skills and talents that you can teach to others. If you were babysitting, maybe you could teach the child how to tie his or her shoes, or how to read a clock. Maybe you know how to play a song on a keyboard, or how to cook something. Is there a craft or hobby you are good at? Can you help someone learn multiplication facts? Can you count to ten in another language? Do you throw well? Try to fill in the callouts below with the variety of skills and talents that you possess.

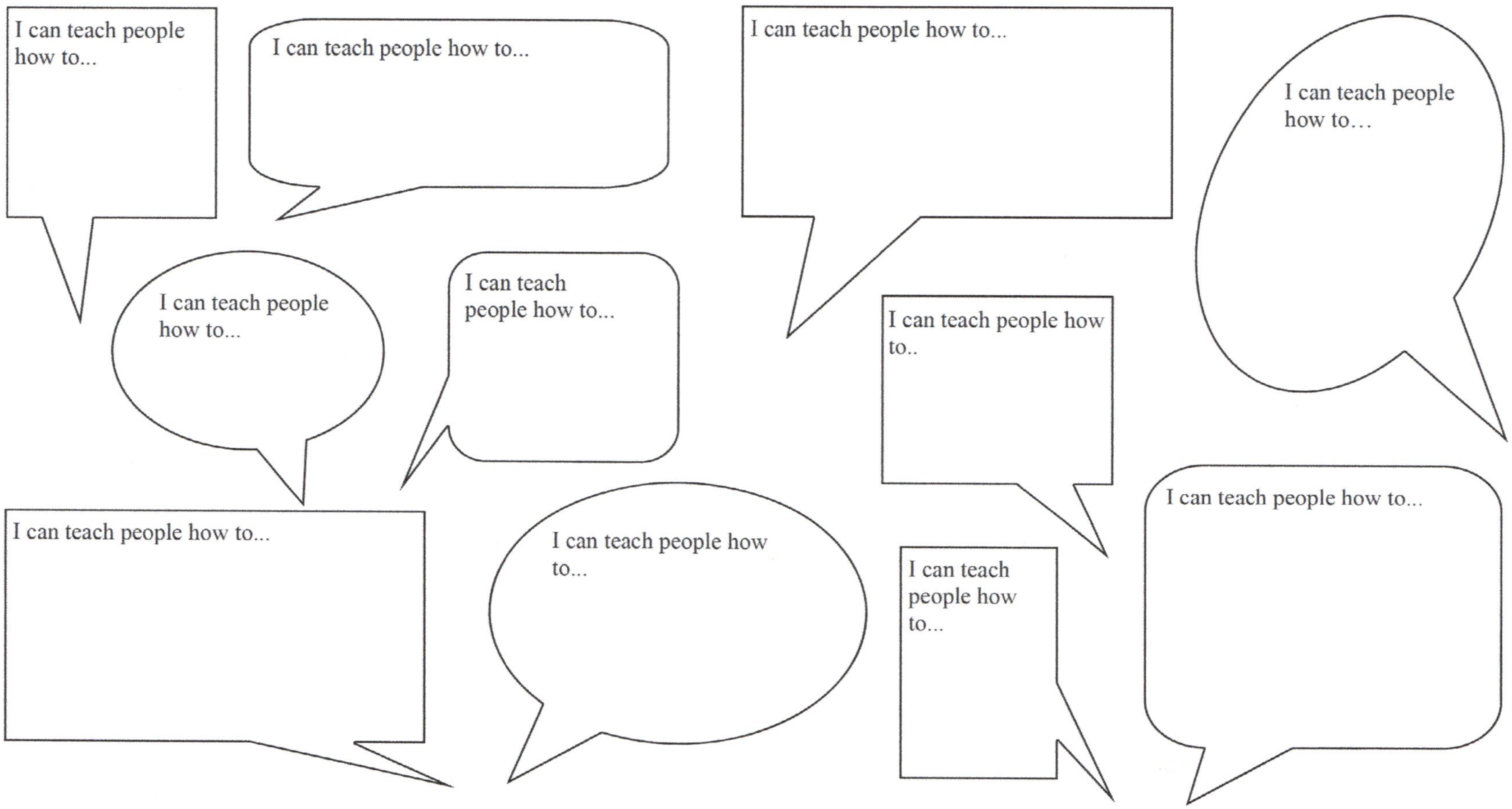

I can teach people how to…

I can teach people how to…

I can teach people how to…

I can teach people how to…

I can teach people how to…

I can teach people how to…

I can teach people how to…

I can teach people how to…

I can teach people how to…

I can teach people how to…

I can teach people how to…

I can teach people how to…

I can teach people how to…

MY RELATIONSHIPS

It's normal to think about only ourselves, but actually you are a part of many separate relationships. Each relationship is special in its own way. Check which relationships you have, and give the names of the people involved. Add any additional relationship categories that you can think of:

I AM...

_____ the daughter or son of _____ .

_____ a sister or brother to _____ .

_____ the grandchild of _____ .

_____ the great-grandchild of _____ .

_____ a niece or nephew to _____ .

_____ a great-niece or nephew of _____ .

_____ a cousin to _____ .

_____ an aunt or uncle to _____ .

_____ a pet owner of _____ .

_____ a neighbor to _____ .

_____ a friend of _____ .

_____ a student of _____ .

_____ a boyfriend or girlfriend to _____ .

_____ a church member of _____ .

_____ a team member of _____ .

_____ a club member of _____ .

_____ a volunteer at _____ .

_____ a babysitter of _____ .

_____ an acquaintance of _____ .

_____ _____ of _____ .

_____ _____ of _____ .

CHAPTER 1 ~ PERSONAL MATURITY

MY SUPPORT SYSTEM

On the previous page you listed several of the relationships you have with people in your life right now. Most of the people and pets you named can help support you through both difficult and happy times. List the names on or near each person or pet who supports you. Think about who acknowledges your special days, like birthdays and school performances. Add facial features, hair and names of the people and pets in the drawing. Feel free to cross out or add people and pets.

HOLIDAYS, ANNIVERSARIES, & BIRTHDAYS!

It's nice to know when the holidays occur during the year. Those dates are listed below. Easter and Hanukkah aren't listed, because the dates vary from year to year. Ask your friends and relatives when their birthdays and anniversaries are, and then use this page as a handy place to keep track of those important dates.

January
1-New Year's Day

Martin Luther King, Jr. birthday-3rd Monday

February
14-Valentine's Day

President's Day—3rd Mon.

March
17-St. Patrick's Day

April
1-April Fool's Day

May
Mother's Day-2nd Sunday

Memorial Day-observed on the last Monday

June
Father's Day-3rd Sunday

July
4-Independence Day

August

September
Labor Day-1st Monday

October
12-Columbus Day

31-Halloween

November
11-Veteran's Day

Thanksgiving-4th Thursday

December
25-Christmas

31-New Year's Eve

CHAPTER 1 ~ PERSONAL MATURITY

ADULT INTERVIEW

WHAT WAS IT LIKE FOR MY PARENT, GUARDIAN OR GRANDPARENT WHEN HE OR SHE WAS MY AGE?

It might be fun to learn about what your parent, guardian, grandparent, or other adult went through when they were your age. Sit down and have an interesting discussion with one of them. Use these questions, and any other questions that might come to mind as a guide.

1. What were you like when you were my age? Were you outgoing? Quiet? Active?

2. Did you have to do any chores? What were they? Were you paid to do them?

3. How well did you do in school? What was your favorite subject? Your least favorite?

4. Were you involved in any school or community activities?

5. How did your parent(s) or guardian(s) discipline you when you did something wrong?

6. If you had siblings, did you get along with them?

7. What did you think about most of the time?

8. What was going on in the world around you when you were growing up?

9. What would you change about your childhood?

10. What is one of your fondest childhood memories?

11. Other questions:

MY PERSONAL ACROSTIC

Use the space below to write your first name in large letters, vertically, along the left side of the paper. Then, use each letter of your name to start a word, or phrase, that describes you. Here is what it might look like for someone named Chris:

Cool.

Has a good sense of humor.

Really wants to be a musician someday.

Is smart.

Someone you would enjoy knowing.

CHAPTER 1 ~ PERSONAL MATURITY

COMPLIMENTS

Use the Compliment Log on the next few pages to record any *pats on the back* you've been given. Maybe a parent or teacher has complimented you, or maybe someone who met you for the first time said something that made you feel good inside. Try to recall any compliments you've received in the past, and record them in your Compliment Log. Compliments can come in a variety of ways. People might say something to you about your *personal* self, (this chapter relates to that); your *emotional* self; *social* self; *intellectual* self; *physical* self; or your *ethical* self. You'll understand more about those areas after you have gone through this book.

If you can't think of any compliments you've been given so far, go to your parent or guardian, or any other adult who knows you well, and ask that person to write in your log. A good friend would be another source to try.

HERE'S AN IDEA!

You could make your own separate *Compliment Book*.

Buy a small composition book. Cover the front with words and pictures that represent you. Magazines and computer graphics are fun to use for this activity. As you go through life, use the book to include not only the nice things that people have said to you, but also any letters, cards or emails that make you feel good inside.

CHAPTER 1 ~ PERSONAL MATURITY

COMPLIMENT LOG

On _____ (date), _____ said (or wrote)
this to me: _____
_____ .

It made me feel _____
_____ .

On _____ (date), _____ said (or wrote)
this to me: _____
_____ .

It made me feel _____
_____ .

On _____ (date), _____ said (or wrote)
this to me: _____
_____ .

It made me feel _____
_____ .

CHAPTER 1 ~ PERSONAL MATURITY

COMPLIMENT LOG

On _____ (date), _____ said (or wrote)
this to me: _____
_____ .

It made me feel _____
_____ .

On _____ (date), _____ said (or wrote)
this to me: _____
_____ .

It made me feel _____
_____ .

On _____ (date), _____ said (or wrote)
this to me: _____
_____ .

It made me feel _____
_____ .

CHAPTER 1 ~ PERSONAL MATURITY

WHAT AM I GOING TO DO WHEN I GROW UP?

It's important to know what your loved ones think you might be good at doing for a living someday, since they know you best. Ask your parent(s) or guardian(s), teachers, friends, and other relatives what job they think you might be suited for in the future. Have them tell you why they feel that job path would be a good one for you to take.

Name of Person	Job Suggested	Why they feel I am suited for this type of job:

CHAPTER 1 ~ PERSONAL MATURITY

MY BUCKET LIST

Directions: Begin a list of things you would like to accomplish before you leave this world, or *Kick the Bucket.* That is why this is called a "Bucket List." It might be an odd thought for right now, but take it seriously. Would you like to travel to a foreign country? Get a college degree? Meet a certain public figure? Learn a language? Keep adding to this list as you go through life. It's never too early to start focusing on your long term goals.

CHAPTER 1 ~ PERSONAL MATURITY

MY ACHIEVEMENTS SO FAR...

Stop and think about it—you have accomplished a lot of things so far in your short life! You've learned to crawl, walk, and speak a language, right? Did you learn how to swim? Tie your shoes? Ask your parent or guardian for help coming up with some of your big accomplishments. How have you helped others? Have you won any races? Given a speech? Are you the household checkers champion? Can you beat Aunt Mary in ping pong? Brag it up on the empty scrolls below.

CRAWLING!

WALKING!

CHAPTER 1 ~ PERSONAL MATURITY

MY TIMELINE!

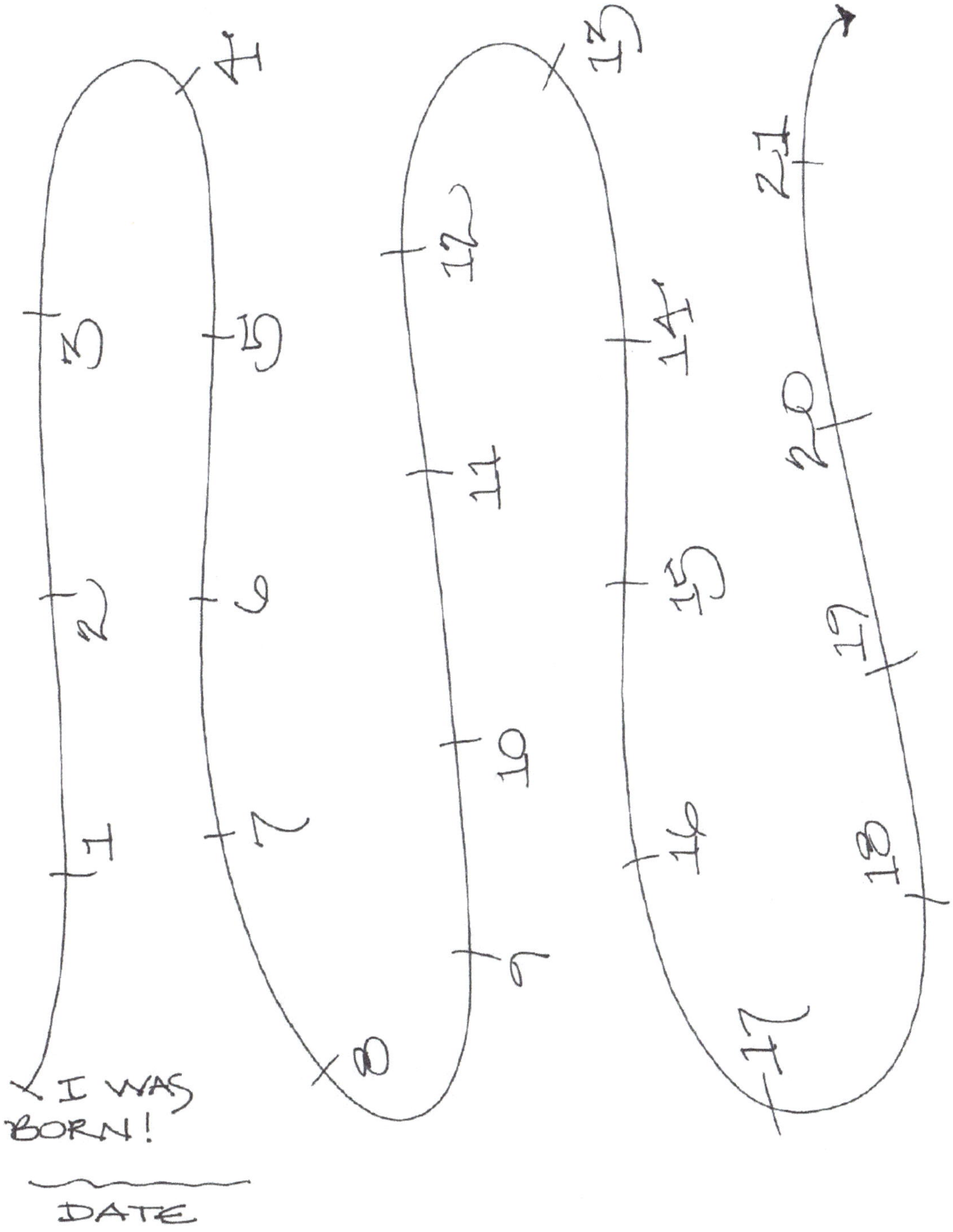

I WAS BORN!
DATE

Use this page to write down all of the important events that have taken place in your life. You probably don't remember what happened before you were 3 or 4, but your relatives can probably fill you in on what took place. Try to think broadly about where you lived, what pets you had, and what important experiences took place. Then, when you get to the age you are now, try to make predictions about the later years, on up to when you turn 21!

INSPIRATIONAL THOUGHTS FOR PERSONAL MATURITY

Now that you have experienced the chapter on Personal Maturity, and learned about taking better care of your personal health, look over the following thoughts, or quotes, and highlight the ones that inspire you.*

- Notice the good in you.

- Never let anyone or anything make you feel less than you are.

- Destiny is not a matter of chance; it is a matter of choice.
  —William Jennings Bryan

- Don't ask others to do things for you that you can do for yourself.

- Loving yourself will allow others to love you.

- Find more than one thing that works for you.

- Others will love you if you love you.

- You get out of life what you put into it.

- It's never too late to be what you want to be.

- Even when no one else does, believe in yourself.

- Failure is an event, not a person.

- Life is a mirror and will reflect back to the thinker what he thinks into it.
  —Earnest Holmes

- Just as it's impossible for people to agree on 'the best movie or book of all time'; a single definition of beauty doesn't exist. —Shari Graydon

- If not now, then when will you?

* Authors of quotes are listed when known

MORE INSPIRATIONAL THOUGHTS FOR PERSONAL MATURITY

Use the rest of this page to write other thoughts or quotes relating to your personal health, that you either create or discover throughout your life.

- It's never crowded along the extra mile.

- Do not give up, the beginning is always the hardest.

- It's not a question of can you, but will you?

- You don't always get what you wish for, you get what you work for!

- You must do one thing you think you cannot do. —Eleanor Roosevelt

- If you run into a wall, don't turn around and give up. Figure out how to climb it, go through it, or work around it. —Michael Jordan

- No choice is also a choice. —Yiddish proverb

- Nobody can make you feel bad about yourself unless you let them. —Eleanor Roosevelt

- A pessimist sees the difficulty in every opportunity; an optimist sees the opportunity in every difficulty. —Winston Churchill

-

-

-

-

-

PERSONAL GOALS

Now that you've gone through the chapter on Personal Maturity, perhaps you are interested in setting a goal for yourself, so you can become even more awesome! Suggestions are listed below, but you probably also have some pretty good ideas of what you want and need to work on when it comes to improving how you feel about yourself.

Give it some thought, and consider using a chart, like the one on the next page, or making one of your own. Draw stars or place stickers on days when you have accomplished your goal. Hopefully you won't need a tangible reward for accomplishing your goal. After all, it should simply feel good inside when you are working on bettering yourself.

- Create a "Compliment Book" similar to the one discussed in this chapter.
- Use page 16, *Holidays, Anniversaries & Birthdays*, to find out everyone's birthdates and anniversaries. Then, create cards for a few of them.
- Pick up your room every night before bed, for one week.
- Do your chores every day for one week without being reminded.
- Start a journal where you compliment yourself every night on three things you did well that day.
- Interview your parents, guardian, or grandparents about your ancestry.
- Make a collage, about people and things you like, using computer images or old magazines. Put it up on your wall, in your locker or on your binder.
- Every time you catch yourself putting yourself down, make yourself stop and give yourself two 'put ups'.
- With parent or guardian permission, try doing one new thing a week that you have never done before.
- Get up 15 minutes earlier each day and take more time getting ready for school.
- Try giving a sincere compliment to one person each day.
- Your ideas:
-
-

CHAPTER 1 ~ PERSONAL MATURITY

MY PERSONAL GOAL

MONTH _____

Sunday	Monday	Tuesday	Wednesday	Thursday	Friday	Saturday

I will try to _____

at least _____ times a week. If I am successful for _____ weeks in a row, I will feel _____.

If you don't achieve your goal, no worries. Just try again, or "tweak" your goal to make it more achievable.

CHAPTER 2

EMOTIONAL MATURITY

About Emotional Maturity

Are you a worrier? Or, are you cool, calm and collected? Some people seem pretty calm on the outside, but are hurting inside. This chapter will help you discover and display more of your feelings and help you think more positively about the world around you, and your future within it.

It's important for all of us to take care of our mental health, because depression is such a widespread problem. Some people are genetically more prone to having fragile mental health, so learning more about yourself, and how you can prevent becoming depressed is even more important.

When something is troubling you, sometimes it's good to ask yourself: "Will it really matter a month from now? A year from now?" This can help you keep it all in perspective. Try to live one day at a time, and not worry so much about the future. Hopefully you'll find some good activities in this chapter that can help you with your emotional maturity.

SIMPLE PLEASURES

Sometimes you probably notice events happening around you that put a smile on your face, or touch your heart. Try to keep a log, here and on the next page, of those "Simple Pleasures" that you notice as you go through life. Be aware of how these events affect your senses. Bring the list to mind during times of stress. It will help you relax, and not take life too seriously. Some examples are listed for you, to help get you started.

I RELISH THE SMELL OF

- The Thanksgiving turkey.
-
-
-
-
-

I APPRECIATE THE SIGHT OF

- A baby asleep on his parent's shoulder.
-
-
-
-
-

SIMPLE PLEASURES

I SAVOR THE TASTE OF

- A new fun flavor of ice cream.
-
-
-
-

I ENJOY THE FEEL OF

- Getting into a bed with fresh clean sheets.
-
-
-
-

I AM DELIGHTED BY THE SOUND OF

- A sprinkler on a warm day.
-
-
-
-

CHAPTER 2 ~ EMOTIONAL MATURITY

VISUALIZING MY OWN SPECIAL PLACE

Daydreaming can be a good outlet for people. Remember not to let it distract you though! This is an exercise in imagining a stress-free place to go to mentally, when you need a little break. You get to design and visualize a special room that is all yours. Use the questions on this page to help you imagine just the right place, and then use the next page to sketch what you have created in your mind. Come to your own conclusion of what you'd like your special place to look, smell, sound and feel like.

- Where do you want this special place to be? Is it in a tree house? At the ocean? In the mountains? On a houseboat on a lake? In a forest?

- How do you enter it? Through a door? A tunnel? Do you climb up a ladder to a tree? Is there an elevator?

- What colors do you see on the walls? What other colors do you see around you?

- Are there windows? What shapes are they? What do you see outside the windows? Can you see the stars at night?

- What kind of flooring is there? A rug? Or, is there something else instead, like grass? Water? Snow? Sand?

- Is there anything on the walls? Pictures? A TV? Speakers?

- Is there a bed? A hammock? A tent? Are there pillows? Where do you sleep?

- Are there any pets? What kind? Colors? Names? Is there a fish tank?

- What other furniture is there in your special place? A comfy chair? What kind? Does it recline? Swivel? Is there a bookcase full of books? A piano?

- Is there a desk? A computer? A file cabinet? A Large white board?

- What is the lighting like? Is there a fireplace? Track lighting? Candles?

- Is there a kitchen? Refrigerator? Microwave?

- What are some of the sounds you hear? What does it smell like?

- What do you see yourself doing? Napping? Writing? Reading? Watching TV? Petting your animals? Looking out the window?

CHAPTER 2 ~ EMOTIONAL MATURITY

MY SPECIAL PLACE

Draw the special place that you visualized while following the directions on the previous page.

MY DREAMS

Use the clouds to write down dreams that you remember. They'll be fun to look back at later in life. You could also take a blank notebook, decorate the cover, and make it into a *Dream Journal* that you can use over the years to come. Put it next to your bed, so you can write down a dream as soon as you wake up, before you forget what it was about.

CHAPTER 2 ~ EMOTIONAL MATURITY

BLAST AWAY BOREDOM!

Boredom is one of the biggest challenges kids face during the summer months. It's important to try to motivate yourself to be productive and creative, and to use your time well. Studies show that one of the main reasons why young people turn to drugs is because they are bored. Don't let it happen to you!

It's time to make the following list of...

THINGS TO DO WHEN I'M BORED:

_____
_____
_____
_____
_____
_____
_____
_____
_____
_____
_____
_____

Check the Appendix, pp. 170-172 for a list of over 100 suggestions!

MAYBE IT'S TIME TO START THINKING ON THE POSITIVE SIDE WITH...
AFFIRMATIONS

Do you use your inner voice to talk negatively to yourself? If you do, it's time to learn about: Affirmations.

An affirmation is a positive statement that you need or want to remember about yourself, and about life. It's a way of changing your thinking from the negative side to the positive side, with the use of repetition and visualization.

Here's an example: You might be someone who puts yourself down when you make mistakes. In that case, you might choose an affirmation that says, *I am lovable even when I have a problem or make a mistake*. Because, after all, everyone makes mistakes. Plus, you are awesome, and no one is just like you.

There are several examples of affirmations on the following three pages. Try to find one or more that you would like to start believing more about yourself. Write it on a sticky note and put it where you'll see and read it often. You could place it on your mirror, binder, locker, or on the kitchen cupboard.

Be creative and display affirmations any way you'd like! If you don't want to use sticky notes, you could make large banners and put them up on your wall. Go for it! Use your creativity. Select the phrases that you want to work on. If you don't see a choice that suits your needs, make up your own affirmation.

Everyone doesn't have to love me.	It's OK if I make a mistake today.
I AM RESPONSIBLE FOR HOW MY DAY GOES.	I can handle it when things go wrong.
Not everyone acts or thinks the same.	I can tolerate the people and things that I don't like.
I will give everything my best effort today.	I can control my actions.

I can become all that I choose to be.	I am in charge of everything I learn.
MY LIFE AND ALL THAT I MAKE OF IT IS WITHIN MY POWER.	I can tolerate those around me who might think or act differently.
I must love myself first in order to be in control of my life.	There are people in my life who care about me very much.
I am lovable even when I have a problem or make a mistake.	I am bigger than any of my fears.

I am unique. No two people see the world the same way.	I CAN MAKE SOMEONE'S DAY BY CHANGING HOW THAT PERSON SEES HIMSELF.
I can make things happen.	My mental health is just as important as my physical health.
I am kind.	I am honest.
I am not perfect.	Money and material items are NOT what make people happy.

CHAPTER 2 ~ EMOTIONAL MATURITY

Cut out this section for the doorknob.

<---- Cut this slit to easily hang on your doorknob.

PLEASE KNOCK

and wait for my answer before entering.

Thanks,

The Management

MY PRIVACY SIGN

Would You Like to Have a Little More Privacy?

Cut out this sign and put it on your bedroom doorknob. Or, use it as an example, and make your own sign! Be sure you know your parent or guardian will agree with what it says. You need to show respect in order to receive respect.

PROBLEM-SOLVING PRACTICE

It can be difficult sometimes to make a decision, especially if you are being pressured by a person or a group of people. Remember that you are in charge of yourself, and responsible for your own actions. Try not to fall into doing things just to please others. It's best to think for yourself, and act according to the values you have established for yourself and how you want to live your life. Your parent or guardian is a good resource for you when it comes to establishing your values.

Don't hesitate to take some time making a decision when you are confronted with a problem to solve. Here is one way you can try to work out a solution to a problem:

1. Write out the problem: _____.

2. Make a list of possible solutions, and then brainstorm the pros and cons of each choice:

Possible Solutions	Possible Good	Possible Bad
I could _____		
I could _____		
I could _____		
I could _____		

3. Decide which solution you would like to try and why. If it's a big decision that needs to be made, ask for help from a trusted adult. I will try: _____ _____ because _____.

4. Analyze how well things went after you proceeded with your decision. Things went _____. I felt _____.

5. If you had to make that same decision again, would you do the same? _____ If no, what would you have done differently? _____
_____.

CHAPTER 2 ~ EMOTIONAL MATURITY

WOULD I LIKE TO GET RID OF A BAD HABIT? TRY SOMETHING NEW?

IF YOU ANSWERED, "YES" TO EITHER OF THOSE QUESTIONS, THEN IT'S TIME TO TRY:

21 DAYS TO SUCCESS!

The next page contains a chart that you could use to help start a new healthy habit or to get rid of a bad habit. Studies show that it takes 21 days, or three weeks, of daily effort to stop or start a habit. What would you like to work on? Here are some suggestions:

- Stop biting my nails.
- Walk the dog daily.
- Study or read for one hour daily.
- Stop drinking soda, or limit soda intake to 1-2 per week.
- Be nicer to my sibling.
- Make only positive statements to myself and others.
- Brush my teeth at least twice a day.

You might want to make copies of the chart, since the rule is that you have to start over whenever you miss a day. If the chart is too overwhelming, try making one of your own showing only one week at a time.

This might be something you'd like to work on privately, or perhaps you'd like to have someone support you through your efforts. Maybe your parent or guardian would like to use a chart like this, too. The two of you could be a support system for each other, and the charts could be on display on the kitchen cupboard.

If it's something you really want to work on, don't give up! Anything worth accomplishing in life takes time and effort. You can do it! Remember? You're AWESOME!

 CHAPTER 2 ~ EMOTIONAL MATURITY

21 DAYS TO SUCCESS

YOU DID IT!

21 · 20 · 19 · 18 · 17 · 16 · 15

Almost there!

14 · 13 · 12 · 11 · 10

You're over 1/2 way there!

9 · 8 · 7 · 6

1/3 of the way there!

5 · 4 · 3 · 2 · 1

Starting Date: _____

My Daily Goal is to: _____

Instructions: Color in a circle, or put a sticker on each day that you are successful in achieving your goal. Remember, it takes 21 consecutive successful days to be able to make a new habit stick, or a bad habit go away.

CHAPTER 2 ~ EMOTIONAL MATURITY

MY PUSHBUTTONS: NEGATIVE AND POSITIVE

Do you feel sometimes like people are trying to "push your buttons"? In other words, do you think people try to say things just to set you off and make you feel sad inside? If so, write what those hurtful words might be inside the "explosion" shapes on the sad person. Are there some things you wish people would say to you that would have the opposite effect and actually make you feel like a star inside? If so, write what those words might be inside the star shapes on the happy person. Remember, you can always use self-talk to talk to yourself in that positive way. No one else knows you quite as well as you know yourself.*

*Don't forget to draw hair on the people so they look more like you!

STRESS BUSTERS

Try some of the following activities to help you relax when pressure starts building up inside of you. Check each one off as you give it a try.

- Read a book _____ ❑
- Call a friend, or write in a journal _____ ❑
- Go for a walk, run, or a bike ride _____ ❑
- Massage your neck, back and shoulders, or ask someone to help you _____ ❑
- Do something with your hands, like using a hammer and nails; drawing; painting; or using Play-Doh®. _____ ❑
- Scream into a pillow _____ ❑
- Read a joke or comic book _____ ❑
- Sit in a tree and read, or study nature _____ ❑
- Listen to music, especially a CD of nature sounds _____ ❑
- Ask yourself, "What could be worse?" Or, "Will it really matter a week from now?" (A year from now? Five years from now?) _____ ❑
- Close your eyes and think about some of the "Simple Pleasures" that you listed earlier in this chapter. _____ ❑
- Take a slow deep breath. When you exhale, try to relax your body like a rag doll. Give yourself an affirmation that will help you cope. You can choose one from the pages earlier in this chapter. Repeat 3-5 times. _____ ❑
- Make a list of things to do and decide which item should be a priority. Focus only on that, and let the rest go. _____ ❑
- Punch your pillow and say out loud what is bothering you. _____ ❑

CHAPTER 2 ~ EMOTIONAL MATURITY

STRESS BUSTERS

Fill in the shapes below with more ideas of how to deal with stress in a positive way:

RELAXATION TECHNIQUES TO TRY

If you get to the point where you know you need to chill for awhile, try one of these techniques. Try several of them over time, and see which one best fits your likes and needs. Remember, relaxation doesn't always come easily, so don't give up if a certain technique doesn't work the first time. Any new skill takes practice. Remember to check them off as you go along. ☑

1. **Autogenic Relaxation**—When something is autogenic, it comes from within. So, take yourself on a relaxing journey in your mind. Lie down in a quiet setting and try to focus on controlled breathing. Breathe in for 5 seconds, and then take 5 seconds to exhale. While breathing, concentrate on a peaceful setting. Maybe you visualize the special place you created in this chapter. Or, you could just picture yourself floating on an air mattress at a lake, in the warm sun. ☐

2. **Progressive Relaxation**—Perhaps this is something you've heard of before. After getting into a relaxed state, begin concentrating on tensing and then releasing the tension in each muscle group. Progress from the toes to the legs, stomach, and so on, as you move up the body. Or, start at the top of the body and work your way down. Tense for five seconds and then take about 30 seconds for the release and relaxation of the body part. ☐

3. **Visualization**—This is similar to some of the suggestions in the first method, where a picture of a relaxing setting comes from within your mind. In this method, however, you concentrate on all of your senses. For example, lie down and visualize yourself at a beautiful place, such as the beach. What do you hear? Smell? See? What does it feel like? Can you taste the salty air? ☐

4. **Music**—This one is obvious, of course, and could be used alone, or with any of the previous techniques. Pick something you enjoy listening to, but make sure it gives you a relaxed feeling. Try classical music, it might surprise you how relaxed it can make you feel. There are several choices at your local library. Try to keep worries from creeping into your mind while listening. Just lie there, listen, and concentrate on relaxing your breathing, your muscles, and of course your mind. ☐

5. **Yoga**—You never know if this is something you'll like until you try it! Look for a DVD, or a program on TV. The library probably has exercise DVDs for check out. Other types of exercise that include relaxed movements and breathing are Pilates and Tai Chi. ☐

6. **Massage**—It is costly to pay for a professional massage. But, you can always try self-massage. Concentrate on each body part, similar to the progressive relaxation technique listed above. This time, instead of working on tensing and releasing without touching the muscle group, try massaging the tension out of that area. Don't forget these all-important areas: the neck; the lower back; and the area between the shoulder blades. If you can't reach the area between the shoulder blades, ask for help from your parent or guardian. ☐

7. **Affirmations**—Look over the three pages of affirmations in this chapter. Pick out one that suits your needs, or think of something that is troubling you, and turn it into a positive statement. Instead of, "I have no friends," try, "I am worthy of someone's friendship." Repeat the affirmation several times in your mind while relaxing to music, or in a quiet room. ☐

CHAPTER 2 ~ EMOTIONAL MATURITY

GRIEVING THROUGH LOSSES

Have you ever misplaced something very important to you, (like the stuffed animal your parent gave you when you were young), and had a feeling come over you that you may never see it again? There is a *grieving* process that people go through when they experience a 'loss'. A loss is something that has happened in your life that has caused you grief, or sadness, whether on a very small scale, (such as losing your favorite pencil), or on a grand scale, such as the death of a loved one, or the family pet.

Everyone grieves differently—sometimes you might go through the process very quickly; sometimes you might get 'stuck' on one of the stages; sometimes you might skip one or more of the stages; and, sometimes it can take years to get to the final stage of grieving. Often the intensity and duration of the grieving process has to do with how many losses you've already grieved over or how close or special the person or item was to you.

Look over the list of losses below, and check off which ones you have already been through. Some of them won't seem like anything to have had to grieve over, but most of the changes, or new experiences that we go through, whether big or small, can be an emotional experience. Change is often difficult to go through at first, but can wind up having some positive effect, after a period of time. For example, you might not want to move to another neighborhood or city, but in the end you might eventually appreciate the new friends you've made, and the skills you've gained, such as being able to make friends more easily.

_____ Entering Kindergarten   _____ Divorce of Parents

_____ Moving   _____ Death of a Pet

_____ Being Bullied   _____ Loved One's Addiction*

_____ Losing a Favorite Item   _____ My Own Illness or Condition

_____ Loss of Financial Support   _____ Loved One's Illness

_____ Getting Detention or Suspension _____ Poor Test Scores

_____ Entering Middle School   _____ Argument With Someone

_____ Losing a Friend   _____ Loss of Contact With Parent

_____ Death of a Loved One   _____ Being Grounded

List other topics you can think of: _____ _____

_____ _____   _____ _____

*In this case, it is usually the loss of hope that a person will grieve over.

THE STAGES OF GRIEVING

Here are some of the stages of grieving. See if you can relate to them, as you think about some of the losses you have already experienced. Then, you will have a chance on the next page to analyze how you grieved over one of your losses.

1. SHOCK. When you first encounter a loss, or even the anticipation of a loss, you might feel numb inside. You might cry a little, or you might wonder why you can't cry.

2. DENIAL. This often happens right along with the first stage. You don't and won't believe the sad event is happening, or going to happen.

3. ANGER. A person experiencing a loss often feels that life is unfair. Well, that's true. Life isn't fair. In this stage you probably feel angry that something bad is happening. During this stage, a person might take his/her anger out on someone or something else. There's a term for that, it is called *displacement*. Have you ever been so angry that you yelled at someone? Slammed a door? Hit a pillow? That's displacement. Anger is one of the stages of grieving that a person can get stuck on. Sometimes it takes talking with a health professional to help move through this stage of grieving.

4. GUILT. Sometimes this is called the, "If only…." stage. The person experiencing the loss might blame himself for not doing more to prevent the situation from ever happening. It's normal to feel some guilt, but it is necessary to let it go and move on. There's never a good reason to beat yourself up over a situation. It doesn't do any good. Things happen. No one can control everything.

5. DEPRESSION. This is another one of the stages that someone can get stuck on. The person might need help from a health professional, and maybe even medication, since serious depression can actually change brain chemistry. It's normal to feel sad about bad things that happen in your life. But, it can be harmful to hang onto those sad feelings for an extended period of time. Talking to an adult you trust can help get you through this stage. Some people find it helpful to journal about their feelings. Finally, time can help the pain go away, and the sadness can be replaced with fond memories, and a new outlook on life.

6. TEARS. Perhaps there have already been some tears along the way, but this is more like, "The Big Cry." Sometimes it is in the form of a scream or an angry outburst. And, as with the other stages, it can be skipped altogether. If you do experience this stage, it can be quite a feeling of relief, letting out all those pent up feelings.

7. GROWTH. At this point you accept the loss and gain *resiliency*, the ability to bounce back from future losses more easily.

CHAPTER 2 ~ EMOTIONAL MATURITY

ANALYZING A LOSS

It can be very healing to try to go over something that has happened in your life; to look more closely at how you went through it; and to look at what you gained from that experience. Try to think of one of the losses you checked off earlier, and write it out below. Then, try to describe how or even if you went through each of the stages of grieving. You might also want to talk with your parent or guardian about a loss he or she has had, and ask that person to share the various feelings he or she went through while grieving over the loss. It can be a learning experience, and a bonding experience for the both of you.

MY LOSS: _____

1. SHOCK.
Did I feel numb? How did I react to the news? _____
_____

2. DENIAL.
Did I face the facts, or did I deny this was happening at first? _____
_____

3. ANGER.
Did I have any anger? Did I take it out on anyone or anything? Describe. _____
_____

4. GUILT.
Did I blame myself at all? If I did, what did I say to myself? _____
_____

5. DEPRESSION.
Was I sad? How did I act? What did I feel? What did I say? _____
_____

6. TEARS.
Did I have a big cry, scream or outburst of any kind? How did it feel? _____
_____

7. GROWTH.
Did I finally accept the loss? _____ What did I gain from having gone through this experience? _____

CHAPTER 2 ~ EMOTIONAL MATURITY

TURNING AROUND NEGATIVE SELF-TALK

This page would be a good one for adults as well as for kids. It's something many of us need to work on: We need to stop putting ourselves down! What's that all about? We should be our own #1 fans. After all, no one knows a person better than he or she knows himself or herself. It's pretty tough to try to love others if you don't love yourself first. So, try turning the following negative statements into positive ones. See if you can make the transition from sounding like a pessimist to sounding like an optimist.

The first one is done for you:

Negative: I'm so stupid. I can't believe I just did that.

Positive: I'm not stupid. I just need to slow down and think before I act.

Negative: I can't do anything right.

Positive: _____

Negative: I'm never going to learn this.

Positive: _____

Negative: I hate my (you fill in the body part) _____.

Positive: _____

Negative: Nobody likes me.

Positive: _____

Negative: I can't control myself when I'm angry.

Positive: _____

Negative: I'll never get anywhere in life.

Positive: _____

Fill in the last one with a thought that you are struggling with and need to turn from negative to positive:

Negative: _____

Positive: _____

CHAPTER 2 ~ EMOTIONAL MATURITY

CELEBRATING THE GOOD CHOICES I HAVE MADE IN MY LIFE

You have made many good choices in your life, one of which is using this book in an effort to become a healthier person. Use this page to brag about those choices you have made in your life that have made you a more well-rounded and happy person. Ask your parent or guardian to help you with this if you have trouble coming up with ideas.

CHAPTER 2 ~ EMOTIONAL MATURITY

JOURNALING

Use this page and the next two pages to write down your thoughts and feelings. You could also draw pictures or doodle.

CHAPTER 2 ~ EMOTIONAL MATURITY

JOURNALING

CHAPTER 2 ~ EMOTIONAL MATURITY

JOURNALING

Consider purchasing a blank book that you can use for future journaling or sketching.

INSPIRATIONAL THOUGHTS FOR EMOTIONAL MATURITY

Now that you have experienced the chapter on Emotional Maturity, and learned about taking better care of your mental health, look over the following thoughts, or quotes, and highlight the ones that inspire you. Authors of quotes are listed, when known.

- Start happiness from within.

- Ask yourself...Does it really matter?

- Accept the problem and you'll soon find the answer.

- Being able to control yourself is a sign of maturity.

- Enjoy yourself in a life of your choosing and a world of your making.

- Don't spend time worrying about things you can't do anything about.

- Happiness is created, not found.

- Say that you need love.

- Optimists keep raincoats handy.

- Asking for support is the first sign of courage.

- Your life is like a canvas...make sure you paint yourself a whole lot of colorful days.

- We do not remember days, we remember moments. –Cesare Pavese

- It isn't the great big pleasures that count the most, it's making a great deal out of the little ones. –Jean Webster

- Remember, danger is just one letter away from anger.

MORE INSPIRATIONAL THOUGHTS FOR EMOTIONAL MATURITY

Finish this page with other thoughts or quotes relating to mental health, that you make up or discover throughout your life.

- Everything is going to be alright. Maybe not today, but eventually.

- People are just as happy as they make up their minds to be.

- If people could make me angry, they could control me. Why should I give someone else such power over my life? —Benjamin Carson

- The odds are very good that worrying is a waste of time. And besides, worrying won't change what happens anyway, will it? —Judie Angell

- When one door of happiness closes, another opens; but often we look so long at the closed door that we do not see the one which has been opened to us.— Helen Keller

- Everyone has different problems, but everyone has some kind of problem.— Justine Rendal

- There is no sight so ugly as the human face in anger. —Louise Fitzhugh

-

-

-

-

EMOTIONAL GOALS

Now that you've gone through the chapter on Emotional Maturity, it's time to consider whether or not you want to set a goal for yourself, so you can work on self-improvement in this area. Everyone should work on self-improvement, as they go through life. There is no end to trying to improve, no finish line. Plus, along the way, you might just inspire others with your confidence or your determination. Some suggestions are listed below. Maybe one of these suggestions will spark an idea within you. Remember that goals should be specific, and something that can be measured or observed. You might want to make a chart for yourself, or a journal, or use the calendar on the next page, to help you keep tabs on yourself. If you don't see a choice that fits your needs, make up one of your own.

- Choose three affirmations from pages 40-42. Make yourself say them three times every morning and three times every night, for three weeks. Be sure to put them up where you'll see them often.

- Ask 5 people what some of their "Simple Pleasures" are, and record them on pages 33 and 34.

- Try two or three of the relaxation techniques listed on page 50.

- Try 10 of the ideas you listed on page 38, *Blasting Away Boredom*. Or try 5 of those ideas, plus 5 ideas from the list in the Appendix, pages 170-172.

- Try to start a good habit, or stop a bad habit. Aim for 5 days in a row, and then work your way up to ten days in a row. If you make it to that point, you'll be ready to use the 21-day chart on page 46.

- Keep a journal of, *Things I am Grateful For*. Write in it every night for eight out of ten days.

- Make yourself a "Dream Journal". Decorate the cover and keep it at your bedside, with a pen. Write in it every day, as soon as you wake, even if you are recording that you don't remember your dream that day.

- Go to the library with the mission of trying to find items that can help you relax more. Find classical music to listen to while reading or studying. Look for books about dealing with stress that are written for kids your age. And, don't forget to check in the audio visual department for a DVD that teaches yoga, Tai chi, or Pilates. Have fun!

- Can you think of any more emotional goals you could try?

CHAPTER 2 ~ EMOTIONAL MATURITY

MY EMOTIONAL GOAL

MONTH _____

Sunday	Monday	Tuesday	Wednesday	Thursday	Friday	Saturday

I will try to _____ _____ at least _____ times a week. If I am successful for _____ weeks in a row, I will feel _____.

If you don't achieve your goal, no worries. Just try again, or "tweak" your goal to make it more achievable.

CHAPTER 3

PHYSICAL MATURITY

CHAPTER 3 ~ PHYSICAL MATURITY

ABOUT PHYSICAL MATURITY

Obviously you are maturing physically on your own. You are going through the changes your body goes through as you develop into a young adult. You are probably going through, or will soon go through puberty. This book will not deal with that type of physical maturity. There are well-written books specifically on that topic. However, what is included in this chapter will certainly help you with your overall physical maturation.

This chapter deals with five main topics: your safety, posture, becoming more active, eating right, and getting enough sleep. All of these topics will certainly help you develop physically into a healthy happy young adult.

This chapter is so critical, given the problems in our country with obesity, eating disorders, and lack of activity. The time is now to develop positive lifelong habits when it comes to how we treat our bodies. You only have one body—take care of it. You are awesome, and should treat yourself as such.

CHAPTER 3 ~ PHYSICAL MATURITY

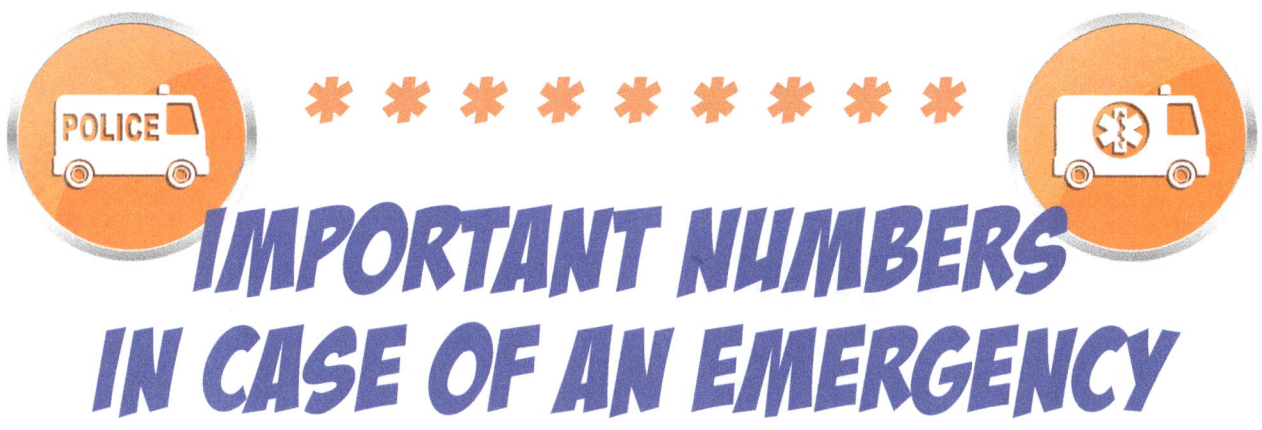

IMPORTANT NUMBERS IN CASE OF AN EMERGENCY

Part of being physically mature is to make sure that you are keeping yourself safe at all times. Fill in this form and place it where you and your family can locate it easily. Don't forget to put the contacts into family cell phones, too.

Relatives to Call:

Name: _____ Number: _____

Name: _____ Number: _____

Name: _____ Number: _____

Veterinarian:

Name: _____ Number: _____

General Doctor:

Name: _____ Number: _____

Eye Doctor:

Name: _____ Number: _____

Dentist:

Name: _____ Number: _____

Neighbor:

Name: _____ Number: _____

Family Friend:

Name: _____ Number: _____

Other:

Name: _____ Number: _____

SAFETY SURVEY

An individual's safety practices could include a variety of topics. This survey does not cover everything you should be thinking about, but it's a start. Score yourself this way:

- 2 points = This happens all of the time.
- 1 point = This happens some of the time.
- 0 points = This never happens.

_____ The floor to my bedroom is not cluttered.

_____ If I walk outside at night, I make sure to have someone else with me.

_____ I wear a lifejacket while in a boat.

_____ I wear a helmet (and fasten the straps!) every time I ride a bike or a skateboard, or if I rollerblade.

_____ I drink plenty of water, especially before, during, and after exercise.

_____ I wear sunscreen, with a protection factor of at least 30, whenever I am out in the sun or the snow.

_____ If I dive into water I make sure the water is deep enough, and that my parent or guardian approves.

_____ When I use fireworks, I have adult supervision.

_____ When I walk, or ride a bike, scooter or a skateboard, I follow the traffic signals and all of the rules of the road.

_____ I carry emergency numbers with me.

_____ I am an assertive person and can say 'No' to friends who try to convince me, or dare me to do something I know I should not do.

_____ I do not think that it is my job to talk to a stranger who appears harmless and simply wants to ask for directions.

_____ I lock doors and windows when instructed to do so by my parent or guardian, and whenever I am babysitting.

_____ I think before I do anything.

_____ I do not give out personal information about myself or my parent(s) or guardian(s), unless I have their approval.

_____ I do not use a sexually suggestive screen name.

_____ My parent or guardian approves of all the sites I visit online.

_____ I do not post a picture on any social media site without approval from my parent or guardian.

_____ I am not a cyber bully. I do not spread rumors or post anything hurtful online.

_____ If I am angry with someone, I discuss it calmly, or seek help to resolve the situation.

_____ If I have thoughts of hurting myself or someone else, I seek the help of my parent or guardian or a school counselor.

How did you do? Total your points. The author feels that:

- 39-44 total points = Good Job!
- 33-38 points = You're on your way!
- 27-32 points = Kind of shaky!
- Less than 27 points = Uh oh. Time to make some changes!

Accidents are the #1 Cause of Death in Children and Adolescents.
Be Safe!

AM I GETTING ENOUGH SLEEP?

Did you know that sleeping is the most important part of your day? Well, at least it is when it comes to allowing the brain to process the information that you took in during the day. You wouldn't want to short change all the learning that took place during the school day by not getting enough sleep, would you? Plus, growth hormone is released when you sleep! It wouldn't be a very good idea to mess with that important process. Studies show that children ages 7-12 need 10-11 hours of sleep a night. Just in case you need some help getting a good night's rest, here are some ideas to try. Check them off after you've tried them.

- ☐ Keep the room dark. Consider wearing a mask.
- ☐ Try taking a warm bath before bed. 
- ☐ Try using an orange bulb in the bedside lamp. 
- ☐ Stop all elecronics one hour before bed — read instead. 
- ☐ Work out before 7 PM. 
- ☐ Don't go to bed too hungry or too full. 
- ☐ Keep the same sleep schedule all 7 days of the week. 
- ☐ Try listening to classical music or a CD of nature sounds. 
- ☐ Try drinking hot decaffinated tea in the evening. 
- ☐ Keep the room at a cool temperature. Try a fan. 
- ☐ No food or drink containing caffeine after 2 PM. 
- ☐ Change sheets every week.

CHAPTER 3 ~ PHYSICAL MATURITY

HOW GOOD IS MY HYGIENE?

If you work on taking care of yourself and your personal health needs, others will perceive you as being clean, healthy, confident and happy. On the other hand, if you walk around with greasy hair, or in dirty clothes, or not smelling very good, it will be hard to be accepted as the awesome person you are. That's why it's important to put your best foot forward. Put forth your best effort to be the best you can be, and see how good it feels physically and mentally.

Check off the habits you already have. At the end, count how many items you've checked, and see what your rating is at this point. Then, consider taking on a few of the habits that weren't checked off.

1. I wash my hands and face every night before going to bed. ❏
2. I brush and floss my teeth before I go to bed. ❏
3. I either take a shower or a sponge bath* daily. ❏
4. I shampoo my hair at least every other day. ❏
5. I wash my hands thoroughly, with soap and water, after using the restroom, and before meals. ❏
6. I change my clothing on a regular basis, making sure to always look (and smell) clean and fresh. ❏
7. Before I leave the house, I make sure my face and hands are clean, my teeth are brushed, and my hair is combed. ❏
8. If I have to sneeze (or cough), and I don't have a tissue in hand, I sneeze into the inside of my elbow, so that I am not spreading germs. ❏
9. I keep my nails clean and trimmed. ❏
10. If I am active during the day, I make sure I cool down, and wash my face before returning to normal activity. ❏

Total # of checks: _____

If you checked off **8 or more** items, you're a hygiene star!
If you checked off **6 or 7** items, you're on your way.
Less than 6 items checked? Not sure anyone will sit next to you in class or at the lunch table. Time to work on improvement in this area.

*A "sponge bath" is when you wash your underarms, face, hands, feet and private areas with warm sudsy water from a basin, or sink. Then, empty the basin and fill it with water. Rinse and dry those areas.

CHAPTER 3 ~ PHYSICAL MATURITY

DO I TAKE GOOD CARE OF MY VERTEBRAE?

Well, do you? Here's a checklist. See how many items you can check off. Recent studies show that kids as young as 10 are starting to already have problems with at least one disc in their backs. Behaviors, whether good or bad, that you form early in life can affect your health in a positive or negative way later in life. By the way, your vertebrae are the bones in your spinal column. Your spine has over 30 vertebrae, starting at your tail bone and going up through the neck. It's important to take care of your spinal column by properly developing and maintaining the muscles that help support it.

DO I:

_____ Get at least 30 minutes of vigorous exercise a day?

_____ Wear the backpack shoulder straps properly—one over each shoulder?

_____ Get my vision checked every few years?*

_____ Practice standing up straight, with my shoulders back?

_____ Make sure that my backpack fits so that the shoulders are supporting most of the weight?

_____ Make sure to raise my book to a comfortable angle while reading, so I don't have to bend my head over?

_____ Have such good posture that no one ever says, "Sit (or stand) up straight!"?

_____ Get up and take a 5 minute break for every 30 minutes that I sit?

_____ Do some stretching exercises daily?

_____ Sit in a chair that fits my body size, so that I'm not having to slouch?

_____ Carry no more than 5-10% of my body weight in my backpack?

_____ Try to get most of my work done at school, so that I don't have to bring home so many large textbooks?

_____ Have the computer monitor at a convenient height?

_____ Feel confident and walk tall, with shoulders back and head up?

> **If you checked off at least 11 of the items, you're spinal column is pretty happy with you. If not, then it's time to give your spine more respect!**
>
> *People with poor vision will often strain their necks to see what is not in focus.

AM I A NUTRITION WIZARD?

This is going to be one tough quiz, to see what you really know about eating right. Take the quiz and then check the next page to find out what your score says about you.

TRUE OR FALSE:

___1. A calorie is a measurement of the grams of fat in food.

___2. All kids between the ages of 10 and 14 need pretty much the same amount of calories per day.

___3. A food label does not have to list the percent of fat in the food.

___4. It's OK to eat all foods. Just make sure you eat moderate amounts.

___5. A food label will always list exactly how many calories are in the container.

___6. When you're checking for how much salt is in a food, look for the word "sodium" on the label.

___7. If you are a vegetarian, there are still plenty of protein choices to fulfill your body's needs.

___8. If you don't eat a healthy diet, a daily multivitamin will replace the nutrients that you don't get in the foods you eat.

___9. Saturated fat is the good kind of fat.

___10. Even if you're young and/or thin, you could still be clogging your arteries with cholesterol.

Answers: 1. False 2. False 3. True 4. True 5. True 6. True 7. True 8. False 9. False 10. True

CHAPTER 3 ~ PHYSICAL MATURITY

HOW DID I DO ON THE QUIZ?

8-10 correct = Wiz Kid!

6-7 correct = Need Improvement

Less than 6 = Call 911
 (Just kidding)

Here is an explanation of the answers from the quiz on the previous page:

ANSWERS FOR QUESTIONS 1-4

1. False—A calorie is the measurement of the amount of fuel in a food or drink. The calories in food can come from: fat (9 calories per gram); carbohydrates (4 calories per gram); protein (also just 4 calories per gram); or, alcohol (7 calories per gram). You can see why people sometimes gain weight easily on a high fat diet, since fat has more than twice the calories that are in protein and carbohydrates.

2. False—To say that all kids in a certain age group need the same amount of calories is too general of a statement, since kids come in all sizes and can have such a range of activity levels. Calorie needs are based on gender, height, weight, age, muscle mass, and level of physical activity. This is one reason why a couch potato will gain weight easily. If you don't move much, you don't require a lot of fuel, or calories.

3. True—Labels can be very misleading. It would be better if they DID have to tell you what percent of the food item comes from fat. You need fat, but no more than 30% of what you eat in a day should come from fat. If they had to list the % of fat that's in a food item then you'd know that regular potato chips are about 60% fat, and baked potato chips are only about 13% fat!

What you see on the food labels, is something called % Daily Value. That percentage states how much just one serving of that food item will contribute towards the amount of each specific nutrient you need in one day. To make matters even more confusing, this number is based on a 2,000 calorie a day diet, so it's just an average. You may require more or less calories than that, as you learned in question #2.

4. True!—If people would just get in their heads that anything in excess is opposed to nature, maybe we wouldn't have the obesity problem we have in this nation. You can even get away with eating a small amount of sweets daily, if you eat a variety of foods from the healthful food groups, in moderate amounts.

ANSWERS FOR QUESTIONS 5-10

Isn't she done explaining the quiz answers yet?

5. False—People sometimes glance too quickly at a food label, and assume that the number of calories listed is the precise # of calories they will be eating. But, the number of calories at the top of the label is the number of calories per serving, so it is equally important to look for the number of servings per container. If a chicken pot pie label lists 450 calories per serving, but a serving size was only 1/2 of the pie, and you ate the whole pie, (which is easy to do), then you actually consumed 900 calories. It pays to read food labels carefully.

6. True—Sodium is salt. Some people's blood pressure can be affected quite a bit by their sodium intake. Try not to use salt shakers, since there is so much salt in most of our foods already. Some foods that are high in sodium include: soups, pickles, cheese, chips and pretzels.

7. True—You can choose several foods to provide your protein needs without eating animal meat. Examples of foods that vegetarians choose, containing protein are: nuts (including peanut butter); seeds; eggs; tofu and other soy bean products; cheese, and other dairy products; and dried beans, such as kidney beans, black beans, etc.

8. False—A pill can't provide you with the nutrients your body needs. Remember that your body needs fuel, (calories), and there aren't any significant calories in vitamins. That is not to say that it isn't helpful to have a daily multivitamin, but look at it as only a small supplement to your body's needs, just in case your diet lacks certain vitamins and/or minerals.

9. False—Saturated fat is the type of fat that can clog your arteries, so look carefully at food labels to see how much saturated fat you are getting. Try to avoid it as much as possible. Trans fats are the other fats to avoid. The good news is that there are good fats that your body needs. They are called unsaturated fats, and come from plants, fish, nuts, and other healthy sources.

10. True—Too bad more people don't understand the fact that they can be thin and/or young and still be clogging their arteries. Thin people often think they are healthy, but maybe their food choices are unhealthy. They might not be overweight, but fat can still be clogging their arteries. Someone can also have high blood cholesterol because of genetics, all the more reason to combine exercise with a balanced diet.

HOW GOOD ARE MY EATING HABITS?

Read each statement and assign yourself the following points, according to each of your answers:

That's me! = 2 points.
I'm like that once in a while = 1 point.
I never do that = 0 points.

OK. Let's get started:

____ 1. Most of the time my eating habits are to eat three meals and two snacks a day.

____ 2. I always feel at least a little bit hungry when I eat, and do not feel too full when I'm done with a meal or snack.

____ 3. I drink 6-8 cups of water a day, (not counting liquids that happen to contain water).

____ 4. I limit sugary drinks to no more than one every other day.

____ 5. I read and understand food labels.

____ 6. I have at least three servings of dairy a day. That means three of these one serving choices: one cup of milk; one small container of yogurt; or, one ounce of cheese.*

____ 7. I eat at least three servings of vegetables a day. (One serving is basically one cup of raw, or one half cup of cooked vegetables.)

____ 8. When I eat bread and cereal, it is almost always a whole grain product.

____ 9. I have a few servings of fruit a day, making sure not to have too much fruit juice, since one serving of juice is only 1/2 cup.

____ 10. I eat two or three servings of protein daily.*

Now, add up your points. Here is what your results say about you:

16-20 Points: You're doing great!

12-15 Points: You're on your way.

11 or less points: Time to get serious about your eating habits.

*Check page 177 in the Appendix for: "What Does A Serving Size Look Like?"

HEALTHY SNACKS!

PLACE AN "X" NEXT TO THE SNACKS THAT SOUND GOOD TO YOU!

CRUNCHY:

_____	Teddy Grahams	_____	Graham Crackers
_____	Popcorn	_____	Tortilla Chips and Salsa
_____	Trail Mix	_____	Rice Cakes
_____	Nuts	_____	Bean Dip with Crackers or Chips
_____	Pretzels	_____	Whole Grain Crackers with Hummus
_____	Animal Crackers	_____	Cereal or Granola Bar
_____	Tuna and Crackers	_____	Ricotta cheese on Crisp Bread
_____	Crackers and Cheese	_____	Deli-meat wrapped around a Pickle
_____	Soy Nuts	_____	Raw Vegetables with Hummus
_____	Seeds (Sunflower, Pumpkin)	_____	Celery and Peanut Butter
_____	Baked Chips	_____	Apples and Cheese
_____	Sun Chips	_____	Light Ranch Dressing with Veggies

WARM:

_____	Sugar-free Hot Chocolate	_____	Whole Grain Toast with Peanut Butter
_____	Applesauce	_____	1/2 English Muffin with Melted Cheese
_____	Small Blueberry Muffin	_____	Oatmeal (add cinnamon, raisins, etc.)
_____	Small Burrito or Taco	_____	Cornbread with 100% Fruit Jam
_____	Bran Muffin	_____	Banana, Zucchini or Pumpkin Bread
_____	Cup of Soup	_____	Cup of Chili
_____	Small Baked Potato (with Lowfat Sour Cream or Plain Greek Yogurt)		

CHEWY:

_____	String Cheese	_____	1/2 Bagel with Light Cream Cheese
_____	Raisins	_____	Small Salad (with Light Dressing)
_____	Fruit Rollup	_____	1/2 Sandwich (Chicken, Tuna, Egg)
_____	Banana	_____	Breadsticks (with Marinara Sauce)

MORE HEALTHY SNACKS!

COLD:

_____	Glass of Milk	_____	Hard-boiled Egg
_____	Frozen Grapes	_____	Vegetable Juice (V-8)
_____	Greek or Lowfat Yogurt	_____	100% Fruit Juice
_____	Fruit/Yogurt/Ice Smoothie	_____	Vanilla Soy Milk
_____	Fat-free Chocolate Milk	_____	Cottage Cheese and Fruit
_____	3-Bean Salad	_____	Fruit Salad
_____	Sugar-free Fudgesicle	_____	Fruit Kabob
_____	Sorbet	_____	Popsicle, made with 100% Juice
_____	Light Ice Cream (1/2 cup only)	_____	Sugar-free Jell-O, with Fruit Inside
_____	Nonfat Frozen Yogurt	_____	Low fat Pudding
_____	Berries with Light Cool Whip	_____	Salad (with Light Dressing)
_____	Frozen Banana		

OTHER IDEAS AND COMBINATIONS:

_____
_____
_____
_____
_____

SHOPPING LIST TO SUGGEST:

_____   _____
_____   _____
_____   _____
_____   _____
_____   _____
_____   _____
_____   _____
_____   _____

WHAT DIETARY CHANGES AM I WILLING TO MAKE?

Use the following scoring system to answer each of the following questions. Then we'll see just how willing you are to make some healthy changes in your diet!

4 points = That's what I do, all the time!
3 points = I already do that once in awhile.
2 points = I'll give it a good try.
1 points = I'll only try if I'm bribed!
0 points = No way! Not in a million years!

_____ 1. Would you drink skim milk?*
_____ 2. When ordering a meal, would you substitute salad for fries?
_____ 3. Would you order water or milk at a restaurant, rather than having a soda?
_____ 4. Would you have nonfat Greek yogurt on a baked potato instead of sour cream?
_____ 5. Would you make a sandwich with 100% whole grain bread rather than white bread?
_____ 6. Would you eat baked chips instead of regular chips if you had the choice?
_____ 7. Would you choose whole grain cereal over sugared cereal?
_____ 8. Would you choose a piece of fresh fruit over a glass of 100% fruit juice?
_____ 9. Would you choose water over an energy drink?
_____ 10. Would you eat most of your vegetables raw rather than cooked?
_____ 11. Would you ask for chicken to be grilled rather than fried?
_____ 12. Would you eat a ground turkey burger?
_____ 13. Would you ask for salad dressing to be served on the side instead of on the salad?
_____ 14. Would you be willing to substitute mustard or light mayo for regular mayo?
_____ 15. Would you eat raw rather than roasted and salted nuts?
_____ 16. Would you be willing to eat a vegetarian meal for dinner at least once a week?
_____ 17. Would you be willing to eat at least three servings of vegetables a day?**
_____ 18. Would you be willing to eat three meals and two healthy snacks*** a day?
_____ 19. Would you be willing to write down everything you eat for one day?
_____ 20. Would you be willing to substitute a baked potato for French fries?

How did you do? Add up your points. Here's what your score probably says about you:

40-80 points = Great attitude!
32-40 points = On your way.
< 31 points = Maybe you should take a class about nutrition.

*It's hard to go right to skim or nonfat milk. Try mixing 2% with 1%; then 1% with skim; and then try drinking just skim milk.
**One serving of vegetables would be one cup raw or 1/2 cup cooked vegetables.
***The author feels that a healthy snack would probably be one of the snacks listed on pages 74-75.

CHAPTER 3 ~ PHYSICAL MATURITY

MY FOOD LOG

You might want to make copies of this page before you write on it. Take one day (or more!) and write down everything you eat and drink. This activity will help you have a better idea of the food choices you make in one day of eating. Try to write down the portion sizes of each item, too. Reading food labels will help. There is also a helpful page in the Appendix, titled *What Does a Serving Size Look Like?* When you're done, check out **https://www.supertracker.usda.gov/default.aspx** for more information, and to see how your eating habits match up to the government's recommendations.

BREAKFAST:

MORNING SNACK:

LUNCH:

AFTERNOON SNACK:

DINNER:

DID I HAVE ANYTHING AFTER DINNER?

DID I INCLUDE EVERYTHING I DRANK TODAY, INCLUDING WATER?

WHICH SPORTS AND ACTIVITIES SOUND INTERESTING?

Mark the sports and activities that interest you, and then consider finding out more about them by researching the Internet. Be sure to type your city and state into your search, so you can find local opportunities. Make phone calls and ask questions. Use the next page to take organized notes. Ask your parent or guardian which activities they might be willing to help support as far as cost, gear and transportation. You may need to call the local bus company if transportation is a problem, or carpool with teammates.

_____ Badminton	_____ Rock Climbing	_____ Fishing	_____ Gymnastics
_____ Discus	_____ Shot put	_____ Race Walking	_____ Soccer
_____ Tap Dancing	_____ Snowboarding	_____ Fencing	_____ Pole vault
_____ Martial Arts	_____ Wrestling	_____ Football	_____ Basketball
_____ Volleyball	_____ Racquetball	_____ BMX Racing	_____ Mt. Biking
_____ Long Jump	_____ Lacrosse	_____ Running	_____ Rowing
_____ Cheerleading	_____ Swimming	_____ Cycling	_____ Juggling
_____ Golf	_____ Archery	_____ Tennis	_____ Table Tennis
_____ Hacky Sack	_____ Hurdles	_____ Figure skating	_____ Go Cart
_____ Baseball	_____ Triathlon	_____ Frisbee Golf	_____ Handball
_____ Ice Hockey	_____ Snow Skiing	_____ Wt. Lifting	_____ Join a Gym
_____ Hip Hop Dance	_____ Foosball	_____ Bowling	
_____ Ballet	_____ Softball	_____ Yoga	
_____ Equestrian Skills	_____ Unicycling		

CHAPTER 3 ~ PHYSICAL MATURITY

RESEARCHING LOCAL SPORTS & ACTIVITIES

Use this page after you have gone over the previous page and checked off the sports and activities you found interesting. Your best resources will probably be the Internet, the phone, the local library, and your parent or guardian. This fact finding exercise will help you discover when and where the activities are offered.

Name of Business	Phone Number	Address	Notes about Cost and Hours of Operation

MY PEDOMETER LOG

Pedometers are inexpensive and can be purchased at any sports supply store. A pedometer is a gadget that measures how many steps you take in a day. Just clip it to your waistband. One mile on the pedometer is 2,000 steps. Use this form to log how many steps you take each day. See if you can log five miles in a day—that's 10,000 steps! Maybe your parent or guardian would like to also get a pedometer. You could challenge each other to see who has logged the most steps by the end of a day or a week!

DATE	DAY OF THE WEEK	TOTAL # STEPS	MILEAGE (total # of steps ÷ 2000)

How about making a copy of the "Pedometer Log" on the next page, and putting it up on your kitchen cupboard, or a bulletin board in your room? Make copies for friends and family members. Share the enthusiasm!

PEDOMETER LOG

DATE	DAY OF THE WEEK	TOTAL # STEPS	MILEAGE (total # of steps ÷ 2000)

READY FOR A PHYSICAL CHALLENGE?

Here is a list of challenges for you to try. When you prove that you can perform a task, with a witness, check it off. There is a blank line at the end so you can come up with your own challenge. This is just level one. The next page has tougher challenges, and the page after that is super challenging. Challenge a grownup to try some of these. Everyone should work on their physical health and maturity on an ongoing basis, for a lifetime.

_____ Go up 7 flights of stairs without stopping.

_____ Jump rope 50 times, without a miss.

_____ Walk, non-stop, for 30 minutes.

_____ Jog one half mile, without stopping. (That's 2 times around a regulation track.)

_____ Juggle* a soccer ball three times in a row.

_____ Juggle* a hacky sack three times in a row.

_____ Swim two lengths of a regulation pool, without stopping.

_____ Ride a bike for 5 miles, without stopping.

_____ Hit a volleyball up into the air 5 times in a row.

_____ Make 2 out of 5 basketball free throw attempts.

_____ Control dribbling a basketball, up and down the basketball court, changing hands each time you get to the end of the court, for 90 seconds, no stopping.

_____ Control dribbling a soccer ball with your feet, while running up and down a field, for 90 seconds, no stopping.

_____ Perform two sets of five push-ups, with only a short rest between, with good form.

_____ _____

*When you juggle a soccer ball or a hacky sack, it means that you keep it up in the air without using your hands.

CHAPTER 3 ~ PHYSICAL MATURITY

READY TO RAMP IT UP?

Are you ready to step up the difficulty level? Now that you've completed some of the challenges on the previous page, try these out. Many adults cannot do these challenges. Remember, you need a witness in order to check something off.

_____ Go up 10 flights of stairs without stopping.

_____ Jump rope 100 times, without a miss.

_____ Walk, non-stop, for 45 minutes.

_____ Jog one mile, without stopping. (That's 4 times around a regulation track.)

_____ Juggle* a soccer ball five times in a row.

_____ Juggle* a hacky sack five times in a row.

_____ Swim underwater, the width of a regulation pool, in one breath.

_____ Ride a bike for 10 miles, without stopping.

_____ Hit a volleyball up into the air 7 times in a row.

_____ Make 3 out of 5 basketball free throw attempts.

_____ Control dribbling a basketball, up and down the basketball court, changing hands each time you get to the end of the court, for three minutes, no stopping.

_____ Control dribbling a soccer ball, with your feet, while running up and down a field, for three minutes, no stopping.

_____ Perform two sets of ten push-ups, with only a short rest between, with good form.

*When you juggle a soccer ball or a hacky sack, it means that you keep it up in the air without using your hands.

THE TOUGHEST PHYSICAL CHALLENGE YET!

Go ahead, call the author crazy, but maybe you can even do some of these challenges! Perhaps there are areas where you excel, and some areas where you need to improve. There's always a tougher challenge out there. So, if you do manage to check off any of these items, be sure to aim for the next level of difficulty. You'll be able to come up with what it should be. Or, if you aren't sure, ask someone to help you come up with your next physical challenge.

____ Run up a set of bleachers, and carefully come down, for five minutes, non-stop.

____ Jump rope for 2 minutes, no mistakes, no stopping.

____ Walk, non-stop, for one hour.

____ Enter and complete a 5K run.

____ Juggle* a soccer ball seven times, without a miss.

____ Juggle* a hacky sack seven times, without a miss.

____ Swim underwater, the length of the pool, in one breath. Or, swim ten lengths of a regulation pool, stopping for only a few seconds at the end of each length.

____ Ride a bike for 15 miles, without stopping.

____ Hit a volleyball up into the air 10 times in a row.

____ Make 4 out of 5 basketball free throw attempts.

____ Control dribbling a basketball, up and down the basketball court, changing hands each time you get to the end of the court, for five minutes, no stopping.

____ Control dribbling a soccer ball, with your feet, while running up and down a field, for five minutes, no stopping.

____ Perform three sets of ten push-ups, with only a short rest between, with good form.

---

*When you juggle a soccer ball or a hacky sack, it means that you keep it up in the air without using your hands.

PHYSICAL ACTIVITIES I CAN DO ALONE:

Do you ever find yourself saying, "I'm bored. There's nothing to do"? Well, next time that happens, remember to check out this page in the book. Maybe you'll get inspired to try one of these ideas. Be sure to add your own ideas at the end of each section.

Hit/throw a ball against a wall   Ride a bike or unicycle   Juggle scarves/balls

Shoot baskets   Practice martial arts   Dance   Go for a walk or jog   Jump rope

Go fishing   Skateboard   Hit golf balls at a driving range   Work out at the gym

Practice tumbling   Shoot darts   Yoga or Pilates   Practice cheerleading   Push-ups

Work on volleyball skills   Swim (with supervision)   Calisthenics (like jumping jacks)

Enter a 5K run or a triathlon   Skip rocks on the water   Hula hoop   Lift weights

_____

_____

I COULD ASK A FRIEND TO:

Play two square   Play croquet   Play wall ball   Go bowling   Play Badminton

Go golfing   Hit a volleyball back and forth   Play with a hacky sack   Shoot baskets

Go fishing   Go to a sports camp together   Play tennis   Go for a jog

Play table tennis   Go swimming   Take a class like Pilates or Yoga or Dance together

Go for a bike ride   Enter a 5K run together   Join a sports team together

Throw a Frisbee together   Throw/catch a softball, baseball or football together

Kick a soccer ball back and forth   Take a class on fencing together   Go to the gym

Make up a dance routine together   Play Hopscotch   Join a wrestling club together

Practice lacrosse skills together   Take the dogs for a walk   Go for a long walk

Enter a triathlon together   Take a swimming class together   Take a gymnastics class

_____

_____

INSPIRATIONAL THOUGHTS FOR PHYSICAL MATURITY

Now that you have experienced the chapter on Physical Maturity, and learned about taking better care of your physical health, look over the following thoughts, or quotes, and highlight the ones that inspire you. Authors of quotes are listed when known.

- I wasn't able to get my weight under control until I began to treat myself like I treat others. —Oprah Winfrey
- Nothing looks as good as healthy feels.
- Sports do not build character, they reveal it.
- Do not reward yourself with food. You're not a dog.
- Health is not valued until sickness comes.
- Problems always look smaller after a warm bath and a good night's sleep.
- Anything in excess is opposed to nature.
- Moderation is the key to losing weight and keeping it off.
- Take good care of your body. It's the only place you have to live. — Jim Rohn
- It's never crowded along the extra mile. —Dr. Wayne Dyer
- Eat to live, and not live to eat. —Benjamin Franklin
- There is no remote for life. Get up and change it yourself.
- It's not *will* power, it's *want* power.
- The difference between try and triumph is just a little umph! —Marvin Phillips
- The groundwork of all happiness is health. —Leigh Hunt
- Strive for progress, not perfection.

CHAPTER 3 ~ PHYSICAL MATURITY

MORE INSPIRATIONAL THOUGHTS FOR PHYSICAL MATURITY

Use the rest of this page to write other thoughts or quotes relating to physical health, that you make up or discover throughout your life.

- There's nothing wrong with change, if it's in the right direction. —Winston Churchill

- Clear your mind of can't. –Samuel Johnson

- If you don't make mistakes, you aren't really trying.

- You want me to do something — tell me I can't do it. —Maya Angelou

- Motivation is what gets you started. Habit is what keeps you going. —Jim Ryan

- I've missed more than 9,000 shots in my career. I've lost almost 300 games. Twenty-six times I've been trusted to take the game winning shot and missed. I've failed over and over and over again in my life. And that is why I succeed. — Michael Jordan.

-
-
-
-
-
-

PHYSICAL GOALS

Now that you've learned more about physical maturity, it's time to make some goals specific to what you need to work on. Are you fit, but in need of working on your eating habits? Or, is it vice-versa? Do your fitness habits need an overhaul? How are you doing with your sleep, safety and hygiene habits? There's always room for self-improvement. And, if physical maturity is a weak area for you, then no worries, you can take some baby steps and start the slow but steady uphill climb towards self-improvement. You'll be amazed by how much better you'll feel as you begin to change your state of physical health for the better. There's a calendar on the following page to help you keep track of your goals. Or, you could make your own chart or journal. Here are some suggested goals, to help you start the brainstorming process.

- Brush your teeth at least two times a day, for 21 days in a row.
- Go to bed no later than 9 pm on school nights, for two weeks.
- Record your food intake for three days and then have it analyzed at **https://www.supertracker.usda.gov/default.aspx** to see how you're doing.
- Walk the dog every day, for at least 30 minutes, for 2 weeks.
- Perform 10 push-ups, and 25 sit-ups, during every commercial while watching TV, for five out of seven consecutive days.
- Research a sport that interests you, and see if there are lessons available.
- Practice at least two of the physical challenges daily, until you succeed.
- No soda or other sugary drinks for 5 days in a row.
- Plan and prepare baggies with healthy snacks, for you and your family, every day for one week.
- Try three of the dietary changes from page 76, one per week.
- Keep track of all of your physical activity, for one month, writing down the number of minutes, and type of activity. Aim for at least an average of thirty minutes a day.

Can you come up with any more goals in the spaces below?

_____

_____

_____

CHAPTER 3 ~ PHYSICAL MATURITY

MY PHYSICAL GOAL

MONTH _____

Sunday	Monday	Tuesday	Wednesday	Thursday	Friday	Saturday

I will try to _____

at least ____ times a week. If I am successful for ____ weeks in a row, I will feel _____.

If you don't achieve your goal, no worries. Just try again, or "tweak" your goal to make it more achievable.

CHAPTER 4

SOCIAL MATURITY

ABOUT SOCIAL MATURITY

Is it easy for you to have conversations with people? How do you feel when you have to get up and give a speech? Some of us are pretty calm when it comes to interpersonal communication, and some of us are painfully shy and cringe at the thought of being called upon in class.

This chapter will hopefully help you in your journey to becoming more mature socially. There are pages about becoming a better listener, having good manners, making friends, and more! The bottom line is that if this is your weak area, it's important to work on it, because good communication is the key to so many opportunities. How else will you find a job if you can't talk to people? How will you eventually find a spouse or significant other in your life? The more you try to "put yourself out there" the easier it will become.

Just remember that you are a good person who has something to say. Most of all, the biggest help for the shy person out there is to practice talking to people, and to believe that what you have to say is important. Some people find it helpful to practice talking to a mirror. It could certainly come in handy when practicing to give a speech in school.

MY NEIGHBORHOOD

Pretend you're in an airplane looking down on your neighborhood. Draw your house or apartment, and the other buildings in your neighborhood. Then, draw the people and where they live. Be sure to put their names down, if you know them, so you can look back on it years from now and remember who lived around you. You could even add words that describe each person. Interacting with people in your neighborhood helps you mature socially.

LOCAL ACTIVITIES TO DO WITH FAMILY AND FRIENDS

Try to think of places to go and fun activities to do around where you live. Maybe this chart could even be used for listing some day trips to the beach, an aquarium, or a museum, even if it takes more than an hour to get there. An example has been listed for you. Notice the use of 'NA' (Not Applicable) if the information isn't needed. Good sources for ideas and specific information might be: the Internet, the yellow pages in the phonebook, the public library, the city parks department, friends and neighbors, or the newspaper. Don't forget to ask your family members what they might like to do.

Name of Activity	Name of Park or Business	Phone #	Address	Days & Hours of Operation	Prices
Swinging and playing on the playground	Neighborhood school	NA	NA	NA	NA

GET PEOPLE TALKING

One way to work on social maturity is to try to get people talking about a particular topic. So, why not take a survey amongst your family members, friends, or even people you don't know but would like to know? If this idea interests you, start with family members, and then if it goes well, and you feel confident about it, you can branch out from there. There are a few different ways to do a survey.

You could ask a *close-ended question*, which is a question that requires a simple yes or no answer, or a question that gives the responder answers to choose from. This type of question makes it easy to come up with the results in terms of percentages. For example, if 7 out of 10 people surveyed say that they would not like to have school uniforms, then you could say 70% were against the idea. You could also keep track of the reasons people give for their answers, because it shows that you are a good listener, especially if you repeat the responder's answer while you are taking notes.

Another type of survey question would be the *open-ended question*. With this type of question, the responder gets to come up with his or her own answer. As you write down people's responses, they will probably also want to know what other people had to say. Here are some examples of both kinds of questions. Plus, there is room for you to brainstorm your own topics to consider:

CLOSED-ENDED QUESTIONS
- Do you ever want to be a parent?
- Do you go home after school, go to an activity, or go to some other destination?
-
-

OPEN-ENDED QUESTIONS
- Where do you see yourself in 10 years, and what do you think you'll be doing?
- Do you have to do any chores at home, and if so, what are they?
-
-

RESULTS FROM GETTING PEOPLE TALKING

After reading page 95, if you decide to go ahead and try a close-ended survey, check out the example below, and then there is a form ready for you to fill out, for a question of your own. If you decide to try an open-ended survey, all you need is blank paper, for recording responses.

EXAMPLE : CLOSE-ENDED QUESTION ASKED —

Do you think we should start and end the school day one hour later?

Possible answers, with tally of responses

Yes	**No**	**Don't Care**
ℍℍ ℍℍ ℍℍ	III	II

Out of 20 people surveyed, 15 said yes; 3 said no; and 2 said they didn't care. **That means that: 75% said yes!**

THE CLOSE-ENDED QUESTION I ASKED :

_____

_____ ?

Possible answers, with tally of responses:

Yes	**No**	**Don't Care**
_____	_____	_____
TALLY	TALLY	TALLY

Out of _____ people surveyed, _____ said _____ ; _____ said _____ ;

and _____ said _____ . That means that _____

_____ .

CHAPTER 4 ~ SOCIAL MATURITY

HOW GOOD ARE MY MANNERS?

When you have good manners, you have good etiquette. Take this two-page survey. See which of these actions you already do and which ones you could work on.

DO I...	I do this	I could work on this
Walk to the RIGHT on the street, at the mall and in the hall?		
Open doors for people?		
Look behind myself when going through a door, to see if the door needs to be held open for the next person?		
Sneeze and cough into my elbow so I am not spreading germs into the air?		
Chew food or gum with my mouth closed?		
Keep from talking, or smacking my lips while chewing food?		
Keep from saying, "But,…" after apologizing?		
Look at people when they talk to me?		
SMILE and look people in the eye as I pass them?		
Put things away in the correct place when I'm done using them?		
Pay attention to a speaker by not fidgeting or multi-tasking while he or she is talking?		
Use correct grammar? (Example: Trying not to use slang words or repeating the word "like" in a conversation.)		
Let my parents, or guardians, and grandparents know that I love them?		
Try not to speak in acronyms? (Example: BFF, LOL, etc.)		
Use good posture, especially at the dinner table and in class?		
Avoid sarcasm since it might hurt someone's feelings?		
Think before I say something?		
Introduce myself when I'm around people I don't know?		
Introduce my friends and acquaintances to others in the room?		
Say "Thank you" to anyone who helps me, feeds me, or drives me somewhere?		

More questions on the next page. -->

CHAPTER 4 ~ SOCIAL MATURITY

AND, DO I...	I do this	I could work on this
Take my dirty dishes to the kitchen sink and rinse them?		
Wait to be invited to someone's house? (It's not cool to invite yourself over to a friend's house.)		
Treat my siblings and my friends' siblings with respect?		
Open car doors and pull out chairs for people older than myself?		
Give my elders first choice of where to sit?		
Acknowledge my parent's or guardian's birthday?		
Try not to point or stare at others?		
Try not to tell secrets around others?		
Write a thank you note, or make a call if I receive a gift, and the person who gave the gift was not there to see me open it?		
Compliment others often?		
Avoid putting people down, or laughing at people, including strangers?		
STOP a behavior that annoys someone when I am asked to stop?		
Keep from touching other people's things without their permission?		
Wash my hands after using the restroom and before a meal?		
Try not to be a picky eater, especially when I am a guest at someone's house?		
Cover my mouth when I yawn?		
Look for opportunities to help those around me?		
Avoid asking personal questions, such as how much someone weighs, or how much someone paid for something?		
Push my chair in when I get up from the table?		
Avoid telling jokes that make fun of different groups of people? (Examples: Fat jokes, blonde jokes, etc.)		
Keep from using a phone or other electronics when I should be looking at and listening to the person who is talking to me?		

So, how many things do you already do? _____

How many do you feel you need to work on? _____

A big part of maturing socially is being able to display good manners in public.

HOW ABOUT A SMILE EXPERIMENT?

Never underestimate the power of a smile. Consider taking a day to experiment with smiling at random people and recording their reactions. Go ahead, make someone's day. If they don't smile back, no worries, emphasize the positive!

I made eye contact and smiled at
_____.
(person's name or description)

The response was _____
_____

I made eye contact and smiled at
_____.
(person's name or description)

The response was _____
_____

I made eye contact and smiled at
_____.
(person's name or description)

The response was _____
_____

I made eye contact and smiled at
_____.
(person's name or description)

The response was _____
_____

I made eye contact and smiled at
_____.
(person's name or description)

The response was _____
_____

I made eye contact and smiled at
_____.
(person's name or description)

The response was _____
_____

CHAPTER 4 ~ SOCIAL MATURITY

AD FOR A FRIEND

Just for fun, if you did want to custom order a new friend, what qualities would you be looking for?

I am a _____ person who enjoys: _____,
(Describe yourself)

_____, _____ and _____.
(Name 4 things your enjoy doing)

I am looking for someone who is _____, _____ and _____.
(Describe three qualities of a good friend)

This person **must** enjoy _____, and be someone
(Name an activity)

who values _____ in a friendship. Call _____.
(What is an important quality you value in a friendship?) (Your name)

CHAPTER 4 ~ SOCIAL MATURITY

WHAT WE HAVE IN COMMON, & WHAT MAKES US UNIQUE

This Venn Diagram is pretty self explanatory. Just compare yourself with one of your close friends or relatives. Hopefully you'll be able to list several qualities you have in common, and several qualities that make each of you unique. Stuck? Look at some of the descriptive words you circled on, *How I See Myself*, page 12.

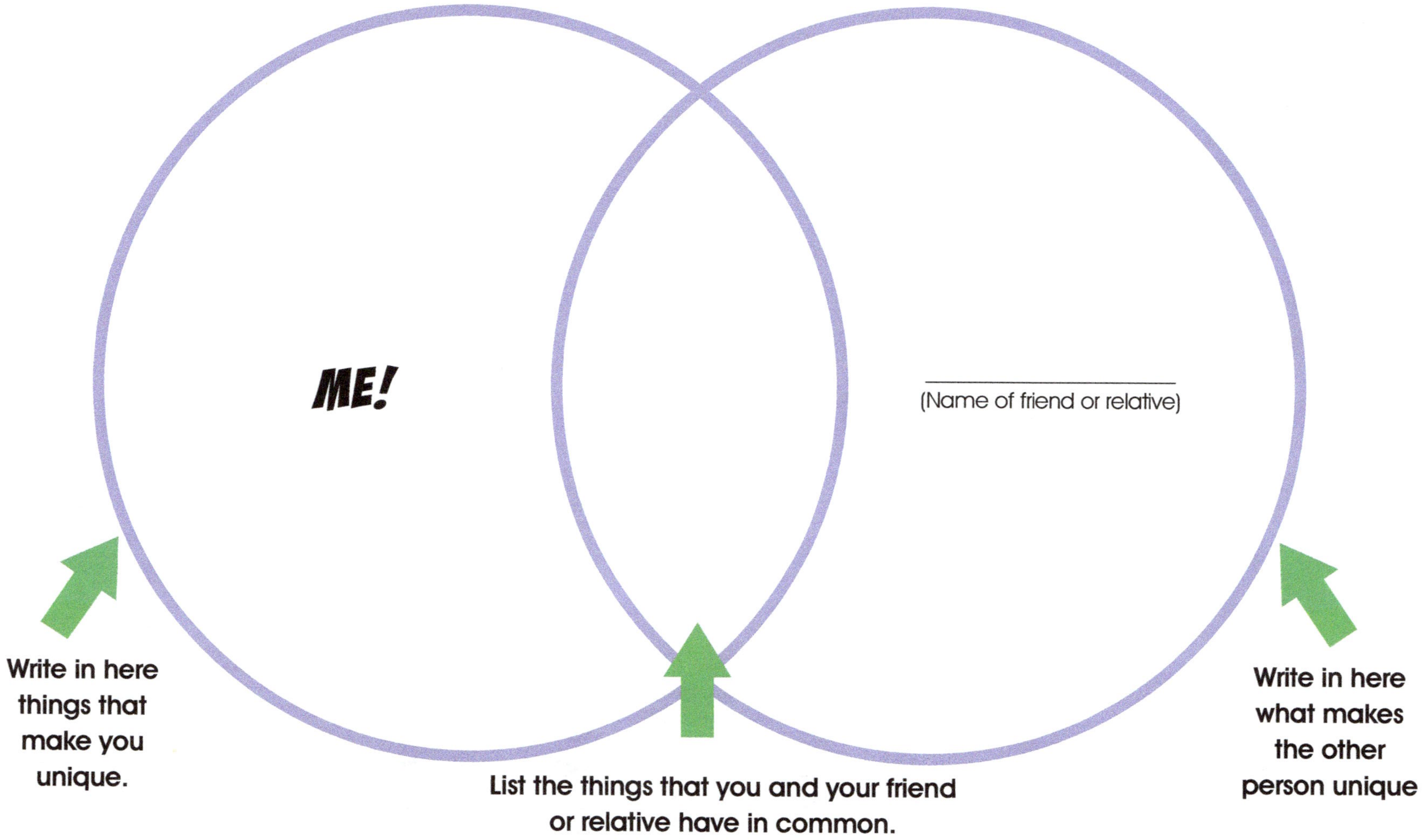

_____
(Name of friend or relative)

ME!

Write in here what makes the other person unique

List the things that you and your friend or relative have in common.

Write in here things that make you unique.

REFUSAL SKILLS

Or…..How to stay out of trouble when someone you care about tries to get you to do something you know is wrong.

Have you ever been with a group of friends, or perhaps just one friend, and a suggestion to do something risky has been made? For example, has someone asked you to try alcohol? Vandalize? Smoke? Sneak out? Skip school? Cheat on a test? Steal? It could be anything that you know could lead to negative consequences. The suggested "trouble" would go against your values, your parent's or guardian's guidelines, or even the law. Chances are that if this hasn't happened to you yet, a risky situation might present itself in your near future. You need to be ready to refuse trouble before it ever happens. If the person suggesting something mischievous is your friend, you could save yourself and that person a lot of heartache, by changing the situation from having negative consequences, to having positive consequences. There are five steps to refusing trouble. Check them out, and then you can practice them on the next page.

STEP 1- ASK QUESTIONS:

As soon as the behavior is suggested by your friend, ask the person why they would want to do that. You could also ask them what they think could happen if you were to get caught.

STEP 2- NAME THE TROUBLE:

Give a serious name to what they are suggesting. For example, if they want you to 'egg' the cranky neighbor's house, tell them, "That's vandalizing." Or, if someone wants you to sneak out with him or her, you could say it is against your parent's or guardian's rules.

STEP 3- NAME THE CONSEQUENCES:

Be very clear about what could happen if you get caught. For example, "I'd be grounded for life!" Or, "We might wind up in detention!"

STEP 4- SUGGEST AN ALTERNATIVE:

Say something like, "I know what we could do! We could ask our parents if we could walk to the mall."

STEP 5- LEAVE:

If the suggestion isn't taken, and the person is still pressuring you, it's time to leave the situation. While walking away, invite him or her to join you if they change their mind.

PRACTICING REFUSAL SKILLS

Before practicing the skills you learned about on the previous page, make a list of healthy and fun activities, (alternatives), that you could suggest to a friend who might pressure you to do something you don't want to do:

Healthy Alternatives: _____

_____

_____

Now, think of a situation that could (or has already) come up with a friend or group of friends. Then, fill in the spaces with what you might say. The situation:

_____

_____

STEP 1-ASK QUESTIONS:

"_____?"

"_____?"

STEP 2-NAME THE TROUBLE:

"That's _____."

STEP 3-NAME THE CONSEQUENCES:

"If we do that, then _____."

STEP 4-SUGGEST AN ALTERNATIVE:

"Hey, why don't we _____ instead?"

STEP 5-LEAVE:

"Well, I'm going to go now. Are you sure you don't want to _____?"

(repeat the healthy alternative)

"If you change your mind, you can catch up with me."

AM I A GOOD LISTENER?

Being a good listener is a sign of social maturity. People will respond to you more positively if you show interest and respect while listening to them, and it will help you later in life making friends, getting and keeping jobs, and improving your intellectual maturity, as well your social maturity. Below is a list of some qualities of a good listener. Check off the ones you know you already practice, and pay close attention to the ones you need to work on.

GOOD LISTENING SKILLS*	I do this	I could work on this
1. Look at the speaker's face and make eye contact.		
2. Do not interrupt the speaker.		
3. Do not fidget or move around when someone is speaking to you.		
4. Have good posture. Shoulders back, chin up, lift the chest a little.		
5. Repeat the message back to the speaker, in your own words. This is called reframing.		
6. Ask questions that show you are interested in what is being said.		
7. If you have a pencil and paper, take notes from what is being said, rather than doodling. Look back up at the speaker often.		
8. If you are listening to someone who is upset about something, try to feel what the speaker is feeling. This is called empathy.		
9. Offer a hug if you feel that is what they need and want.		
10. Nod your head from time to time, so the person knows you are listening, and you understand what he or she is trying to say.		
11. Resist the urge to give advice, unless it is asked for. Understand that the person mostly just needs to talk.		
12. Resist the urge to talk about your own life. You are there to listen and lend support.		
13. Reach out to people, even people you may not know very well, and ask if they'd like to talk about what is bothering them, if they indeed seem upset and need to talk with someone.		
14. Try not to tell someone you know how they feel, because they won't believe you've been through exactly what they are going through.		

* If a friend tells you that he or she wants to hurt himself or herself, or someone else, you must tell a trusted adult.

CHAPTER 4 ~ SOCIAL MATURITY

Make a coupon for a friend or relative for their birthday, or *just because*. Here are some examples, but it would probably be more fun if you make your own. You could even make a coupon book. Examples of what you could put on the coupons would be: a massage; washing the car; yard work; a manicure; fixing a meal; or something clever you come up with on your own. Try to personalize your coupons with what the receiver would really enjoy. Maybe the person would just like some one-on-one quality time with you. It's the thought that counts!

COUPON

Date _____

This coupon entitles _____

to _____

Signed _____

Note: This coupon is not redeemable for cash and cannot be presented with any other offer. Expires on _____

COUPON

Date _____

This coupon entitles _____

to _____

Signed _____

Note: This coupon is not redeemable for cash and cannot be presented with any other offer. Expires on _____

106 CHAPTER 4 ~ SOCIAL MATURITY

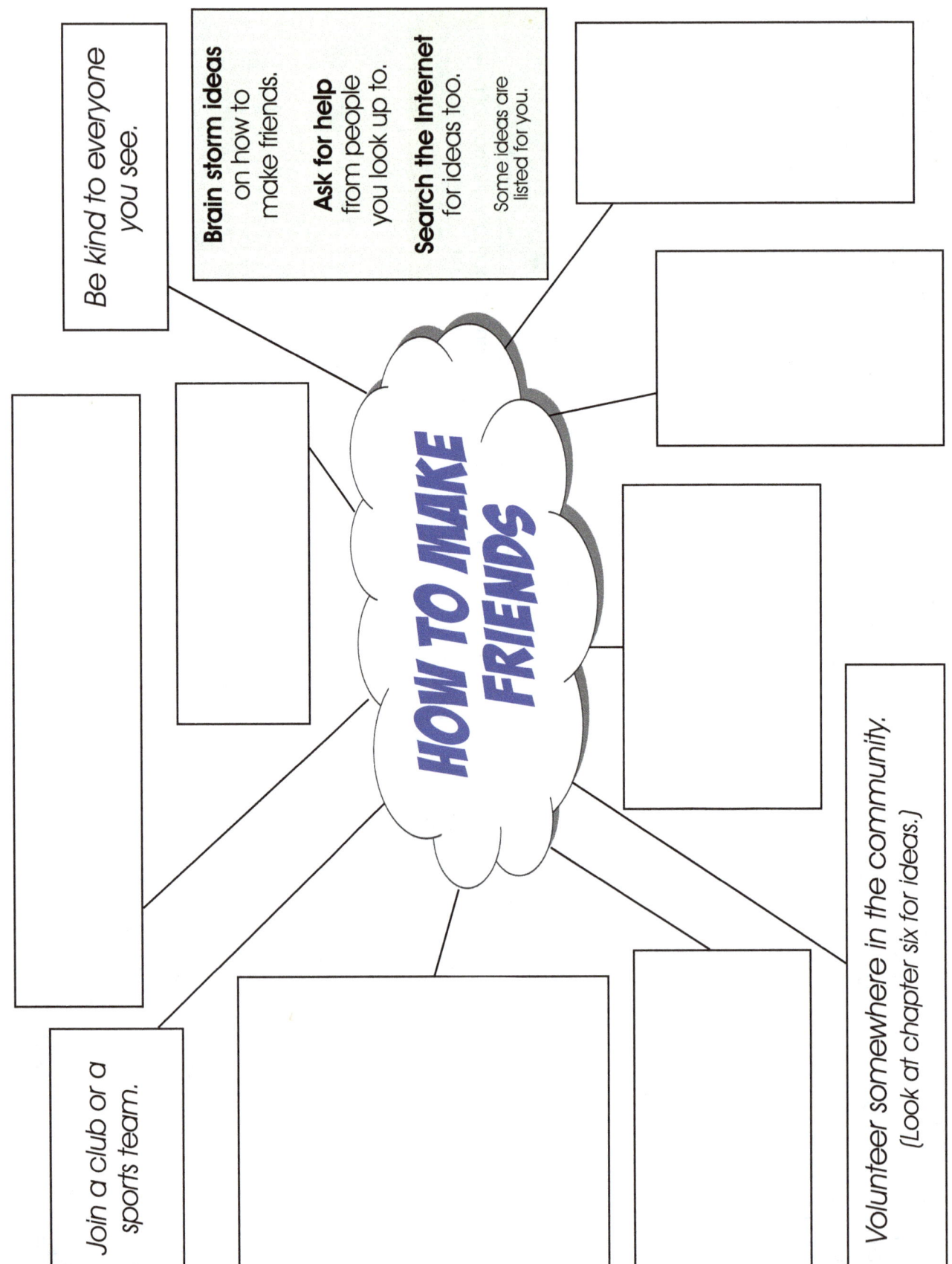

Brain storm ideas on how to make friends.

Ask for help from people you look up to.

Search the Internet for ideas too.

Some ideas are listed for you.

- Be kind to everyone you see.
- Join a club or a sports team.
- Volunteer somewhere in the community. (Look at chapter six for ideas.)

HOW TO MAKE FRIENDS

INSPIRATIONAL THOUGHTS FOR SOCIAL MATURITY

Now that you have experienced the chapter on Social Maturity and learned about taking better care of your social health, look over the following thoughts, or quotes, and highlight the ones that inspire you. Authors of quotes are listed when known.

- Surround yourself with friends who think positive.
- The greatest art of conversation is silence.
- If you can't communicate, you can't run your life.
- Smile with your eyes.
- Don't do for others what they CAN do for themselves.
- Lonely? Call a loved one.
- If you must complain, do it to the person who can help you.
- Don't blame others for your mistakes.
- When it comes to trying to make friends… Not taking risks is a risk.
- Friends are like family you choose.
- Advice from friends is like the weather. Some of it is good, some of it is bad. —Arnold Lobel
- One doesn't know another's sorrow. —Yiddish Proverb
- The only way to have a friend is to be one. —Ralph Waldo Emerson
- Remember that everyone you meet is afraid of something, loves something, and has lost something.
- No one can make you feel inferior without your permission. —Eleanor Roosevelt
- Be kind, for everyone you meet is fighting a hard battle. —Plato

MORE INSPIRATIONAL THOUGHTS FOR SOCIAL MATURITY

Use the rest of this page to write other thoughts or quotes relating to maturing socially, that you make up or discover throughout your life.

- Only equals can be friends. —Ethiopian proverb

- MYOB—Mind Your Own Business.

- Don't shout to prove your point.

- Friendship is born at that moment when one person says to another: "What? You too? I thought I was the only one." —CL Lewis

-
-
-
-
-
-
-
-
-
-

SOCIAL GOALS

Are you already a social butterfly? Even people who are very social can work on improving their level of social maturity. Maybe they aren't good listeners. Or, maybe they could work harder on etiquette. Remember, even though you are already an awesome individual, you can still work on self-improvement. Check out the social goals listed below and see if you might want to try one of them, or come up with a goal or two of your own. Perhaps in all of the six areas of maturity this one is your weakest. Ask an adult who knows you well what they think you should work on. Maybe their love and support is the boost you need, to get out there and become more social. As with the other chapters, there is a blank calendar on the following page in case you need it. Or, maybe you would like to keep a journal or make your own reward chart to better suit your goal. Make sure your goal is specific, and measurable.

- Try the smile experiment for one day, and record the results.

- Ask your parent or guardian if you can plan the next family get-together. Come up with the invitations, menu, place cards, games, etc.

- Sit in a different place when you eat in the school cafeteria, every day, for one week. Write about your observations. Did you talk to people?

- Try not to communicate using text messages for two days in a row, and have real live conversations instead.

- Fill in and present a coupon from this chapter, offering a free service to someone, *just because*.

- Get to know the new kids at school. Help them feel welcome and awesome.

- Practice five of the manners that you checked, *I could work on this*, on pages 97-98. Record your progress.

- If you have siblings, make it a point to be nice to them for three days. Try one of these ideas: help with homework, play outside, or play a board game.

- Write one letter a week to out-of-town friends and/or relatives, for one month. Perform this goal without expecting any return letters, but rather, *just because*.

- Make a list of ideas or favors you can do for family and/or friends, and follow through on a few of them. What is something you can do to please the people or person who helps put a roof over your head?

CHAPTER 4 ~ SOCIAL MATURITY

MY SOCIAL GOAL

MONTH _____

Sunday	Monday	Tuesday	Wednesday	Thursday	Friday	Saturday

I will try to _____ at least ____ times a week. If I am successful for ____ weeks in a row, I will feel _____.

If you don't achieve your goal, no worries. Just try again, or "tweak" your goal to make it more achievable.

CHAPTER 5

INTELLECTUAL MATURITY

About Intellectual Maturity

Don't ever let anyone tell you that you aren't smart. You are smart. You are creative. And, you are awesome.

Perhaps you haven't applied yourself 100%, but you have the capability. You just need to believe in yourself. That's why it's important to work on all six areas of maturity, and not just one.

Have you ever met someone who loved their job? If you have, it's probably because they have a passion for what they are doing. See if you can develop a passion for something that interests you. Then, you can start sharing that passion and you will soon find people will look to you as an expert on that topic. It's as easy as that.

Plus, everyone is creative. Creativity is how you express your own unique ideas. Believe in yourself the next time you are asked to create something. Enjoy it. No one else thinks exactly the same way you do. Now, isn't that awesome?

WHAT GENRE* OF BOOK INTERESTS ME THE MOST?

*Genre is a word that stands for a group of books that share the same style.

First of all, decide if you like *fiction* or *non-fiction* books.

Non-fiction books are based on facts that are known to be true.

Fiction books have at least some elements within them that are made up by the author.

Sometimes people don't read books because they just don't know where to start. Look over the list of book types below and mark the ones that interest you. Then, take a trip to the library, or a bookstore, and consider asking for help finding that genre of book. There are also some very helpful websites that can help direct you to titles of books that your gender and age group is reviewing and recommending. Two such websites are: **www.kidsreads.com** and **www.teenreads.com**.

FICTION:

Realistic _____
Although the story is not something that has really happened, it is written as though it really could happen.

Mystery/Suspense _____

Fantasy _____

Science Fiction (futuristic) _____

Historical Fiction _____
A fictional story that is based on historical events that actually happened.

Folk and Fairy Tales _____

NON-FICTION:

"How to" books _____

Biography _____
This is a story written about someone's life, but is written by someone else.

Autobiography _____
Someone writes about his or her own life.

History books _____

Science books _____

Books on any topic that interests you. _____

CHAPTER 5 ~ INTELLECTUAL MATURITY

EXPANDING MY HORIZONS

The Internet is such a handy and quick source of information. Of course, you have to be careful about your 'searches', making sure a site is reputable and reliable. Instead of learning about just the things that interest you already, why not look into new topics that might interest you? Below are some examples. Mark off the ones you'd like to explore online, and then add some more ideas that might come to you as you read this list. Give it a try. Consider expanding your horizons!

___ Learn about Braille, the alphabet for the blind. How would you spell your name in Braille?

___ Learn about the Morse Code. When is or was it used? How do you spell your name in Morse Code?

___ Learn about sign language. See if you can memorize the American Sign Language alphabet. You can download a free alphabet at **http://www.deafedge.com/**.

___ Find out about your family's medical history. It could have some bearing on your own future health. Look up some of the diseases and conditions that have affected your family members, and find out how you might be able to help prevent them from happening to you. Is there an organization that raises money to help with research for one of the diseases? Maybe you could raise money to help that organization.

OTHER IDEAS:

_____

_____

_____

_____

_____

TIME TO WORK ON STUDY SKILLS!

If you want to work on your intellectual maturity, then you'll need to put a lot of effort into learning more about life and the world around you. Doing well in school should be a priority.

To help you do well in your studies, you will need:

1. A quiet place to study.
2. A designated time to study.
3. To be organized.
4. To have the appropriate materials.
5. Support from loved ones.
6. The desire to do well.

The last need, a desire to do well, will have to come from within. No one can make you want to do well, except for you. That's why it is so important to have self-discipline— the ability and desire to discipline yourself to do well, in all areas of life. Challenge yourself to do the best you can in school, and to be the best person you can be.

The next several pages are designed to help you with the first five items listed above. There's a survey to take, to see what you might already do, and what you might want to start doing; a list of supplies that will help you organize a home study area; a form for listing names of people in your classes who you could call for help with an assignment, or with remembering the details of an assignment; a form for planning long-term projects; a study time/activity planner; and, an example of what a daily agenda notebook might look like. You will probably want to create your own agenda notebook form, so look at the agenda notebook example as a guide to help you design a form that fits your specific class schedule.

SUCCESSFUL STUDY SKILLS

Which of the items listed below are already included in your study practices. Is there anything listed that you'd like to start trying?

Item	I do this	No interest	I'll try it!
I have an agenda notebook that helps me keep track of what needs to be done. (See the example included in this chapter.)			
I have a binder that is organized by subject, has plenty of notebook paper, pens, and sharpened pencils.			
I stop at my locker at the end of the school day to make sure I bring home the necessary books and materials.			
I have a specific study area at home where there are no distractions, such as noisy sibling, TV, etc.			
There is plenty of light in my study area, (both natural light and a lamp).			
I have a calendar on the wall in my study space, so I can keep track of my long term assignments.			
At study time, I make a list of what needs to be done, and then I prioritize the list by numbering the order in which the assignments need to be done.			
The first assignment I work on is the one that is due the soonest. If more than one assignment is due, I work on the hardest one first.			
I study for at least one hour at a time, taking a short 5 minute break once or twice during that time.			
My study time is scheduled, and I study even if I don't have any homework, working on extra credit, reading, or other academic skills.			
When I sit down to study, I make sure I have all the materials I need ahead of time, so I don't have to keep getting up to get things.			
I use a clock, a watch, or a kitchen timer to keep track of how much time I have spent studying.			
I am fit, meaning that I move my entire body at least 30 minutes a day, non-stop. This helps me be alert, and gives me the energy I need.			
If I'm not sure about something, I ask the teacher, a sibling, a parent, or I call someone from my class.			
I take advantage of any study opportunities that are offered either before or after school, such as a study hall, or time in the library.			
I get at least nine hours of sleep a night.			
I eat a variety of healthy foods, in moderate amounts.			
I make sure to have a healthy snack either just before, or during my study time.			

CHAPTER 5 ~ INTELLECTUAL MATURITY

STUDY SKILLS TO WORK ON

Take a look at the items you checked, "I'll try it!" on the previous page, titled *Successful Study Skills*. Write out those sentences below, so you can clearly see what it is you hope to work on. Then, you might want to make one of the suggestions into a goal that you can track on the calendar at the end of this chapter.

If you checked the column titled, "No Interest", write out what it is you are NOT interested in working on, and explain why. Maybe it makes sense to you not to try it for now, but maybe someday you'll look at it again and decide to give it a try. Remember: You're in charge of your own success!

CHAPTER 5 ~ INTELLECTUAL MATURITY

SCHOOL SUPPLIES CHECKLIST!

Below is a list of supplies that might make your life a little easier when trying to study, or put together a project. Some items could be purchased for the household, and some could be purchased for your own study area. Put a check next to the ones you have, and a star next to the ones you'd like to put on a wish list.

_____ pencils-regular	_____ pencil pouch	_____ whiteout
_____ pencil sharpener	_____ notebook	_____ report covers
_____ pencil-mechanical	_____ notebook paper	_____ binder
_____ lead for mechanical pencil	_____ graph paper	_____ dividers
_____ large eraser	_____ hole reinforcements	_____ colored paper
_____ black pen/blue pen	_____ notepad	_____ calculator
_____ red pen	_____ note cards	_____ protractor
_____ bulletin board/thumbtacks	_____ small and large paper clips	
_____ highlighters	_____ binder clips	_____ Post-it® notes
_____ tape dispenser	_____ poster board	_____ compass
_____ tape	_____ scissors with unique edges	
_____ desk	_____ cool paper for backing pictures on posters	
_____ desk lamp	_____ paper cutter	_____ file box
_____ desk chair	_____ computer	_____ files
_____ printer	_____ scissors	_____ white board/pens
_____ print cartridges	_____ glue sticks	_____ weekly planner
_____ printer paper	_____ other _____	_____ other _____

CLASSMATES TO CALL

For Help With Homework Questions

See if you can find someone in each of your classes who is willing to exchange contact information with you, in case you need to ask about the details of an assignment. Not everyone is willing to share their contact information, so don't be offended if someone turns you down. You also might want to check the school's website. Sometimes a teacher will post instructions for assignments and projects.

Subject	Classmate's Name	Phone Number	Email Address

HELP! A PROJECT!

Are you a procrastinator? In other words, are you someone who puts off working on a long-term project until the last minute? Why not try breaking the project down into smaller parts, and put the steps into a logical order? Then, you can cross off the different steps as you accomplish them over time. You never know how well this practice will work until you try it. The experience might prove to be less stressful and the project might be of higher quality.

Title of Project: _____ Due Date: _____

Days I have to work on it: _____

Will I need to do any of the following?

_____ Research online or at the library.
_____ Interview someone.
_____ Take notes in my own words.
_____ Keep track of my references.
_____ Make a poster or some other visual.
_____ Ask someone to edit my writing.
_____ Practice a speech.

What materials do I need? (Think through every step. Do you need a highlighter? Index cards? Poster board? Glue stick?)

Write out a detailed list of what needs to be done, in a logical order, and place a due date next to each step, so you can work on the project gradually, instead of saving everything for the last minute. It would be helpful to have someone check your list, to see if you left anything out.

I need to: Date:

_____ by _____

_____ by _____

_____ by _____

_____ by _____

Write a countdown on your calendar, so you keep track of the # of days you have left.

CHAPTER 5 ~ INTELLECTUAL MATURITY

STUDY AND ACTIVITY PLANNER

Use this form to fill in all of the activities you and your family normally have planned during the week. Then, after you have blocked out times for school hours, meals, chores, youth group, sports, clubs, etc., you can begin to block out study times. Study time should occur daily, unless the goal is to study only on the five school nights. It should be for a minimum of one hour each time. The rule could be that homework is done during that time, but if there are no assignments you would work on math facts, spelling, writing, researching or reading. You will need to make several copies of this page, or perhaps design your own planner. Saturday and Sunday start at 3 PM. on this chart. A chart that you design could have those two days starting earlier, since they are not school days.

Time Period	Monday	Tuesday	Wednesday	Thursday	Friday	Saturday	Sunday
3:00 - 3:30							
3:30 - 4:00							
4:00 - 4:30							
4:30 - 5:00							
5:00 - 5:30							
5:30 - 6:00							
6:00 - 6:30							
6:30 - 7:00							
7:00 - 7:30							
7:30 - 8:00							
8:00 - 8:30							
8:30 - 9:00							

EXAMPLE OF A PAGE FROM AN AGENDA NOTEBOOK

This is an example of how some successful students keep track of what happened during their classes, and whether or not an assignment was given, completed, and turned in. Come up with a system that works for you. For example, in the largest space in the box, write down the topic or learning goal of the lesson. Then, put a check next to the 'Y'* if there's an assignment, and list the specific assignment in the space underneath. Circle the 'Y' when the assignment is completed, and cross out the 'Y' when it has been turned in. Obviously, if there is no homework, you can cross out the 'N' and smile! Don't forget to find out what happened during an absence, and write it into the blank box as well. That way you won't get behind on your work, since you are still accountable for the work you missed.

Monday	Tuesday	Wednesday	Thursday	Friday
MATH: Homework? __Y __N	**MATH:** Homework? __Y __N	**MATH:** Homework? __Y __N	**MATH:** Homework? __Y __N	**MATH:** Homework? __Y __N
ENGLISH: Homework? __Y __N	**ENGLISH:** Homework? __Y __N	**ENGLISH:** Homework? __Y __N	**ENGLISH:** Homework? __Y __N	**ENGLISH:** Homework? __Y __N
SCIENCE: Homework? __Y __N	**SCIENCE:** Homework? __Y __N	**SCIENCE:** Homework? __Y __N	**SCIENCE:** Homework? __Y __N	**SCIENCE:** Homework? __Y __N
SOCIAL STUDIES: Homework? __Y __N	**SOCIAL STUDIES:** Homework? __Y __N	**SOCIAL STUDIES:** Homework? __Y __N	**SOCIAL STUDIES:** Homework? __Y __N	**SOCIAL STUDIES:** Homework? __Y __N
HEALTH: Homework? __Y __N	**HEALTH:** Homework? __Y __N	**HEALTH:** Homework? __Y __N	**HEALTH:** Homework? __Y __N	**HEALTH:** Homework? __Y __N

* Y = Yes and N = No

WHAT ARE MY STRONGEST AREAS OF INTELLIGENCE?

Isn't it great that human beings are not all the same? We all have our own unique genetic makeup, and even our own finger prints, (twins included). Another way that we are different from each other is that we all have different interests and talents. We are all intelligent, yet according to one famous man, Dr. Howard Gardner, we demonstrate our intelligence in different ways, and different parts of our brain could be tied to these different areas of intelligence. It was in 1983 that Gardner, a well-known educator and psychologist from Harvard came up with a *Theory of Multiple Intelligences*.

Basically, Dr. Gardner's theory states that we are all smart, to varying degrees in the following eight ways: verbally, musically, logically, visually, kinesthetically, interpersonally, intrapersonally and naturalistically. Read the descriptions of each type of intelligence, and then try to figure out which areas are your strongest, and which are your weakest. After you read about each area of intelligence, mark the 1-10 spectrum as to how strong you think you are in that area. A score of <u>one means that you are very weak</u> in that area, and a score of <u>ten means you have rock star status!</u>

WORD SMART - ALSO CALLED VERBAL OR LINGUISTIC INTELLIGENCE

This person loves using language in a variety of ways: speaking, reading, writing, listening, playing word games, creating stories, learning foreign languages, etc.

Circle your strength in this area:

    1   2   3   4   5   6   7   8   9   10

MUSIC SMART - ALSO CALLED AUDITORY OR MUSICAL INTELLIGENCE

This person loves listening to music and rhythms, playing music, singing, etc.

Circle your strength in this area:

    1   2   3   4   5   6   7   8   9   10

LOGIC SMART - ALSO CALLED MATHEMATICAL OR LOGICAL INTELLIGENCE

This person loves working with numbers, computers, and scientific concepts; looking at patterns; figuring out riddles, etc.

Circle your strength in this area:

    1   2   3   4   5   6   7   8   9   10

MORE AREAS OF INTELLIGENCE

PICTURE SMART - ALSO CALLED VISUAL OR SPATIAL INTELLIGENCE
This person loves to look at and draw pictures; take pictures; look at (and create) charts and diagrams; describe images, etc.

Circle your strength in this area:

   1   2   3   4   5   6   7   8   9   10

BODY SMART - ALSO CALLED BODILY OR KINESTHETIC INTELLIGENCE
This person loves to move, as in dance and sports, but also likes to create things with his or her hands.

Circle your strength in this area:

   1   2   3   4   5   6   7   8   9   10

PEOPLE SMART - ALSO CALLED INTERPERSONAL INTELLIGENCE
This person is very social, and caring. He or she loves to work with and around other people.

Circle your strength in this area:

   1   2   3   4   5   6   7   8   9   10

SELF SMART - ALSO CALLED INTRAPERSONAL INTELLIGENCE
This person likes to work alone, is often independent, sets goals, and is organized.

Circle your strength in this area:

   1   2   3   4   5   6   7   8   9   10

NATURE SMART - ALSO CALLED NATURALISTIC INTELLIGENCE
This person enjoys looking at and interacting with nature. Areas of interest might be gardening, pet care, and getting involved in taking better care of the world around us.

Circle your strength in this area:

   1   2   3   4   5   6   7   8   9   10

Summarize your answers here, by listing the numbers you circled below each area:

_____ Word Smart	_____ Body Smart	My Strongest Area(s): _____
_____ Music Smart	_____ People Smart	My Weakest Area(s): _____
_____ Logic Smart	_____ Self Smart	
_____ Picture Smart	_____ Nature Smart	

Remember: You already have all 8 kinds of intelligence. You can also work on trying to be a more well-rounded person by working on improvement in all areas of intelligence. Check out the suggestions on the next few pages.

CHAPTER 5 ~ INTELLECTUAL MATURITY

WAYS TO IMPROVE AND ENJOY EACH AREA OF INTELLIGENCE

Put an "X" by the ideas you've already tried. Then, if there's an idea you'd like to try, draw a picture of a light bulb next to it. As you try a new idea, cross out the light bulb.

WORD SMART:

_____ Buy a journal and start writing your own novel or play.

_____ Research a specific topic that interests you.

_____ Start a journal of your writing, picking topics that you enjoy. Try to write every day.

_____ Go to the library and explore. Ask for help if you want to find something specific.

_____ Keep a small notebook of new words that you discover. Write the definitions.

_____ Try storytelling with family members. How about during a road trip? After dinner?

_____ Practice word games, like *Mad Libs*™ or *Scrabble*®. Look for word puzzles, too.

_____ Practice verbal activities: fun words, rhymes, riddles, tongue twisters, jokes, etc.

_____ Join (or start) a book club, or a debate team.

_____ Check the websites of your favorite authors. Consider writing to them.

_____ Look for opportunities to hear a writer speak, or to attend a play.

_____ Look for opportunities to learn words and phrases from other languages.

MUSIC SMART:

_____ Check out and listen to a variety of types of music from your local library.

_____ Experiment with listening to classical music while doing your homework.

_____ Have a sing-a-long with family or friends. Add rhythm from items around the house.

_____ Play musical games with others, like *Name That Tune*, or *Musical Chairs*.

_____ Look for opportunities to listen to live music—concerts, recitals, musicals, etc.

_____ Join a choir or learn to play an instrument, at school or in the community.

_____ Try teaching yourself to play an instrument, such as a harmonica, or a keyboard.

_____ Start a garage band with family and/or friends.

_____ Write or record a piece of music or a rhythm that you create alone, or with a group.

LOGIC SMART:

_____ Play games like chess and checkers—ones that involve using strategy or logic.

_____ Watch the types of channels and shows on TV that focus on science and math.

_____ Work on your mental math. Have family members ask you math problems. Purchase the mental math game called "24".

Adapted from *You're Smarter Than You Think: A Kid's Guide to Multiple Intelligences* by Thomas Armstrong, Ph.D., copyright © 2014, 2003. Used with permission of Free Spirit Publishing Inc., Minneapolis, MN; 800-735-7323; www.freespirit.com. All rights reserved.

LOGIC SMART, CONTINUED:

_____ Visit places (museums, etc.) that have interacting science and math exhibits.

_____ Look for magazines and books that discuss the latest discoveries in science and math.

_____ Look for brainteasers to try. Check websites, library books, and the newspapers.

_____ Research answers to *how* and *why* questions that you've been wondering about.

_____ Ask for parent permission to try some interesting (and safe) science experiments at home.

_____ Ask someone who is good in science or math to explain certain concepts to you.

_____ Try building your own website. Look for instructions on the Internet.

_____ Look into the history of the development of certain math and science concepts.

PICTURE SMART:

_____ Start exploring art books and magazines, or go to an art museum.

_____ Keep a sketch pad with you and draw objects or people that you see.

_____ Collect drawings, photos and designs that you enjoy. Find and decorate a box for them.

_____ Choose a day or an event and take several photos that you then put into a collage or book.

_____ Make your own video, or ask some friends to make a video with you.

_____ Play visual games, like *Pictionary*. Work on puzzles and mazes.

_____ Take an art class at school, or in the community.

_____ Make something out of items you find around the house.

_____ Make an art area in your home, where all of the fun art supplies can be found.

_____ Make a card or write a story using drawings for most of the words.

_____ When reading for content, try drawing pictures of some of the ideas and terms.

BODY SMART:

_____ Learn a new activity that uses hand-eye coordination, such as juggling or table tennis.

_____ Work on your agility with different physical challenges, like the ones on pages 82-84.

_____ Ask people to play charades with you. Look up the rules on the Internet.

_____ Use your hands to create a sculpture using clay, cards, anything you can find.

_____ Learn a new craft, such as quilting, knot-tying, building models, or calligraphy.

_____ Try some of the relaxation activities on page 50.

_____ Try taking a class that focuses on body control, such as dance or martial arts.

_____ Practice being a mime. Act out *everything* you're trying to communicate. No talking!

_____ See if it helps to study while squeezing a soft ball, while standing, or even while moving.

Adapted from *You're Smarter Than You Think: A Kid's Guide to Multiple Intelligences* by Thomas Armstrong, Ph.D., copyright © 2014, 2003. Used with permission of Free Spirit Publishing Inc., Minneapolis, MN; 800-735-7323; www.freespirit.com. All rights reserved.

CHAPTER 5 ~ INTELLECTUAL MATURITY

PEOPLE SMART:

_____ Use pg. 16 to keep track of your friends' and relatives' birthdays.
_____ Make an address book. Include phone numbers and email addresses for everyone you know.
_____ Make a conscious effort to meet and greet new people every day.
_____ Volunteer. Ideas are on pp. 147-149.
_____ Get involved in an activity at school.
_____ Help your neighbors by offering to walk dogs, babysit, or tutor kids.
_____ Design your family tree. Include people's interests, birthdays, anniversaries, etc.
_____ Visit with the elders in your family. Write down some of their stories from the past.

SELF SMART:

_____ Write out your autobiography. Include a prediction of your future as well.
_____ Keep a daily journal, writing down your thoughts, feelings and goals.
_____ Start a "Bucket List", using page 23 in this book.
_____ Decorate your binder, locker or room with pictures and phrases that represent you.
_____ Read a biography about a leader or influential person you admire.
_____ Think about a new skill you would like to learn and figure out how you'll acquire it.
_____ Try to pick up a new habit, or get rid of a bad habit. See pp. 45-46.
_____ Start a journal of famous quotes that inspire you.

NATURE SMART:

_____ Notice and learn the names of the trees and plants that are located near your home.
_____ Plant and take care of flowers, herbs, a tree or a vegetable garden.
_____ Study the constellations and/or the planets. Keep a notebook with pictures and notes.
_____ Find a book about the birds in your area, then find some binoculars and explore!
_____ Go to the library and check out books/magazines about your favorite topic in nature.
_____ Look into volunteering at an animal rescue facility.
_____ Watch nature shows on TV.
_____ What is your favorite animal? Learn as much as you can about that species.
_____ Visit museums that have to do with plants and animals. Go to a zoo or an aquarium.
_____ Look for information about local hiking trails and organize a hike with family.
_____ Start a nature collection. Pressed flowers? Bugs? Rocks?
_____ Look for opportunities to purchase locally grown food. Learn how to cook it!
_____ Look for opportunities to help our environment. Recycling? Join an organization?

DID YOU FIND SOME NEW IDEAS TO TRY? _____

Adapted from *You're Smarter Than You Think: A Kid's Guide to Multiple Intelligences* by Thomas Armstrong, Ph.D., copyright © 2014, 2003. Used with permission of Free Spirit Publishing Inc., Minneapolis, MN; 800-735-7323; www.freespirit.com. All rights reserved.

CHAPTER 5 ~ INTELLECTUAL MATURITY

MOCK JOB INTERVIEW

Time to practice for your future job interview. Have your parent or guardian or a friend ask you some of the following questions, while you sit up straight and pretend to be in a serious job interview. You could either hand this book to your interviewer and allow him or her to jot down notes while you two are talking, or you could skip the interview and fill in the blanks yourself. Either way you approach it, this exercise should help you be a little more prepared when the day comes that you go about seeking your first job. Try thinking of a particular type of job you might be interested in applying for. Will it be in retail? Food service? Working with kids? Inside, at a desk? Mostly outside?

INTERVIEW QUESTIONS:

1. Tell me about yourself. _____
_____.

2. Name some of your strengths: _____
_____.

3. How would these strengths help you in the working world?_____
_____.

4. Name some of your weaknesses: _____
_____.

5. Why do you want this job? _____
_____.

6. What are your educational goals? _____
_____.

7. Where do you see yourself ten years from now? _____
_____.

8. Name a time when you had to make a difficult decision:_____
_____.

9. Have you ever had to lead a group project at school? _____ If yes, what was it, and how do you think you did?_____.

10. Name a time when you set a goal and worked towards it:_____
_____. Were you successful? _____.

11 Name a time in your life when you went above and beyond what was asked of you:_____
_____.

12. Do you have any job experience, (including chores), either paid or volunteer? _____
If yes, please list them:_____.

CHAPTER 5 ~ INTELLECTUAL MATURITY

INTERVIEW QUESTIONS, CONTINUED:

13. How much do you feel you should be paid per hour for this job?* _____
_____.

14. Talk about your proudest achievement: _____
_____.

15. Name someone who has made a big impact on you, and why: _____
_____.

16. What is the title of the last book you read? _____.

17. What do you enjoy doing during your free time? _____.

18. List three words that describe you: _____, _____, _____.

19. How would you deal with an angry customer? _____
_____.

20. What clubs and activities have you been involved in while at school, or in the community? __
_____

21. Is there anything you'd like to add? _____.

Your questions for the employer:

-
-

These are some of the qualities most employers are looking for in a future employee. Circle any of the following qualities that describe you. If there is a quality you'd like to work on, put a star next to it.

Team Player   Leader   Ethical   Intelligent   Punctual

Reasonable   Non-smoker   Patient   Confident   Outgoing

Dependable   Skilled With Computers   Cheerful   Shows Initiative

Loyal   Good Listener   Skilled in a Second Language   Honest

Good Communicator   Has Integrity   Has Good Hygiene

*Look up the minimum wage required by law, by checking online at the US Department of Labor website.

DO I WANT TO RAISE SOME DOUGH?

Wouldn't it be nice to earn a little money of your own to save up for something you've been wanting? Below is a list of suggestions for skills and services that you could offer friends and relatives. Check off the ones you're willing to try, and be sure to add any additional services that you could offer. Then, consider how to market yourself. Will you make a business card? A brochure? A flyer? Will you go door to door? Put up information in the neighborhood? Call your friends? Your friends' parent or guardian? Relatives?

Check out the sample flyer on the next page. It can be a fun and creative venture to make your own marketing materials. The flyer is there just to spark your interest. You decide how you want to present yourself, but be sure your parent or guardian approves of what you are doing. Go for it! You might just be surprised by the positive response.

___ **Babysitting**—Did you know that the Red Cross offers a babysitting course where you can earn a certificate to show your employer?

___ **Pet Care**—-An example of this is in-home care or walking dogs.

___ **Yard Work**—What are you specifically willing to do? Mowing? Raking? Pulling weeds? Watering?

___ **Computer Help**—How about help with other electronics, too? Teach the older generation how to text? How to download tunes?

___ **Wash Cars**

___ **Teach Someone How to Play a Musical Instrument**

___ **Shine Shoes**

___ **Ironing**

___ **Washing Windows**

___ _____

___ _____

CHAPTER 5 ~ INTELLECTUAL MATURITY

SAMPLE FLYER OR BUSINESS CARD

YOUR NAME

PARENT'S OR GUARDIAN'S PHONE NUMBER

Is looking for **SUMMER WORK!** Jobs I can do for you: Mowing, Edging, Other Yard Work, Babysitting, Pet Sitting, Dog Walking, and maybe more! Let's talk!

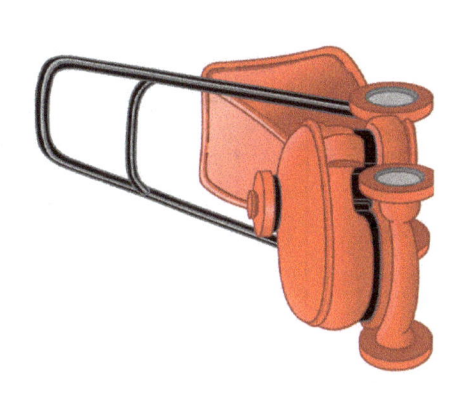

IMPORTANT TIP! Use your parent's or guardian's phone number as the contact number. Be sure to only hand out your flyers or business cards to people you and your parent or guardian know. Never **EVER** give out your address or phone number to strangers.

CHAPTER 5 ~ INTELLECTUAL MATURITY

FUN WITH CARTOONING!

Working on creative projects will help you mature intellectually. Use these cartooning pages to draw your own comic strip. You could make talking bubbles, thought bubbles, or just draw the story without words. Have fun!

CHAPTER 5 ~ INTELLECTUAL MATURITY

MORE FUN WITH CARTOONING!

Here's another blank cartooning page for you to use to create your own picture story. Remember that you can use talking bubbles, thought bubbles, or just draw a story without words. It will be fun to look back at your drawings years from now. Enjoy!

HAVING FUN WITH IDIOMS

An "idiom" is a group of words with a hidden meaning, and is sometimes related to something that happened in history. If you were just learning the English language, most idioms wouldn't make sense to you. It's fun to think about what an idiom would really mean, if it were translated exactly as written.

Below is a list of common idioms. You can find even more online, and you can also research how a particular idiom came about. The next few pages have spaces for drawing some of the idioms. For example, the first idiom is, "I'm all ears!" Draw someone who has ears all over himself. Have fun! This is just another example of how you can exercise your brain and continue to mature intellectually.

IDIOM EXAMPLES YOU COULD DRAW:

- I'm *all ears!*
- Don't *bury your head in the sand*.
- You're just *buttering me up* so you'll get your way.
- Has the *cat got your tongue*?
- I'll *catch you later*.
- It *cost me an arm and a leg*.
- She was *feeling down in the dumps*.
- He had *eyes on the back of his head*.
- They were *fighting tooth and nail*.
- I was *flying by the seat of my pants* to get the project done.
- Get *out of my face!*
- She *jumped down my throat* when she found out about what I had done.
- *Lend me your ear*, please.
- She *jumped out of the frying pan and into the fire*.
- I went *out on a limb* for you.
- It's *raining cats and dogs*.
- He's still *tied to his mother's apron strings*.
- Don't be so *two-faced*.

CHAPTER 5 ~ INTELLECTUAL MATURITY

IDIOMS ILLUSTRATED!

Caption:

Caption:

Caption:

Caption:

136 CHAPTER 5 ~ INTELLECTUAL MATURITY

IDIOMS ILLUSTRATED!

Caption:

Caption:

Caption:

Caption:

CHAPTER 5 ~ INTELLECTUAL MATURITY

DESIGNING MY OWN T-SHIRT!

As you can see, by the previous activities, an enjoyable way to work on developing your intellectual maturity is to do something creative. Use the blank shirts on this and the following page to draw pictures of something specific, or something abstract. If you prefer not to draw, you could write out a statement about yourself, or about life in general. If you *really* like your design, and have some money saved up, you could even take your creation to a T-shirt design shop and have them make the shirt for you! Have fun!

MORE T-SHIRT DESIGNING!

CHAPTER 5 ~ INTELLECTUAL MATURITY

PLAN A PARTY!

Use your creativity to design your own party that you hope to have someday. This helps with social maturity, too. Check the appendix, page 173, for ideas to spark your interest.

Theme: _____

_____

Dress: _____

_____

Decorations: _____

_____

Party Favors: _____

_____

Food: _____

_____

Games: _____

_____

Prizes: _____

_____

Ideas for invitations: _____

_____

Other: _____

_____

INSPIRATIONAL THOUGHTS FOR INTELLECTUAL MATURITY

Now that you have experienced the chapter on intellectual maturity, read over the following quotes related to learning and being creative, and highlight the ones that inspire you the most. Authors of quotes are listed when known.

- Make decisions in the morning. That's when your brain is the sharpest.
- Ideas are one thing, but what you do with your ideas is another thing.
- Education is the difference between what we are and what we want to become.
- IQ will never be as strong as I CAN or I DO.
- Learn five clean jokes.
- Don't ever stop learning.
- If you really want to be smart, learn to listen.
- Sharpen your brain with visualization.
- A book is a friend.—American Proverb
- Know how to do something well to enjoy it. —Pearl S. Buck
- Knowledge is power. —Sir Francis Bacon
- Ashes to ashes. Dust to dust. Oil those brains before they rust.
- Learning is wealth that can't be stolen.—Philippine proverb
- You know, you can learn to do anything if you really want to hard enough. —Janet Taylor Lisle
- To live a creative life, we must lose our fear of being wrong. —Joseph Chilton Pearse
- A mind is a terrible thing to waste.—United Negro College Fund slogan

MORE INSPIRATIONAL THOUGHTS FOR INTELLECTUAL MATURITY

Use the rest of this page to write other thoughts or quotes relating to your intellectual health, that you make up or discover throughout your life.

- We can't take any credit for our talents. It's how we use them that counts. — Madeleine L'Engle

- If you're not prepared to be wrong, you'll never come up with anything original. —Ken Robinson

- Others have seen what is and asked why. I have seen what could be and asked why not.—Pablo Picasso

- Curiosity is one of the most permanent and certain characteristics of a vigorous intellect.—Samuel Johnson

- It is better to have a fair intellect that is well used than a powerful one that is idle.—Bryant H. McGill

- Will and intellect are one and the same thing.—Baruch Spinoza

-

-

-

-

-

INTELLECTUAL GOALS

Within the 6 areas of maturity, intellectual maturity should be the easiest area for coming up with goals. There's so much out there to learn. Plus, creativity is included in this topic. There is no end to how creative you can be. So, pick something you'd really like to learn about, or pick a form of self-expression, and make a specific attainable goal for yourself. Once you've achieved that goal, pick the next step, or go another direction. Some suggestions are listed below—they are there to inspire you to think of some on your own. Remember, you are awesome!

- Try some of the study skills that you marked, "I'll try it," on page 116, *Successful Study Skills*.

- Make agenda notebook pages that fit your class schedule, and bind them together somehow into a notebook. Make extras to share with friends.

- Prepare a flyer, or business cards, in an effort to find odd jobs.

- Work on writing poetry, songs, or a short story. Use the calendar and check off the days you work on it. Tell yourself to write 3-4 days a week.

- Use the calendar as a reading log. Log an average of 30 minutes of reading each night before bed. Get help finding a book that matches your interests.

- Choose a topic that interests you. Research the subject and see if there is a class you can take to learn more about it.

- Start your own comic strip, or joke book.

- Look up which books are top sellers in the genre you enjoy. Then, take a field trip to the library or a used book store.

- Look into a local drama group and see if maybe acting is for you.

- Consider reading to kids at a nearby pre-school.

- Consider starting a club at school. Talk to an adult who might help you.

- Look for a variety of leadership opportunities at school, church, or in the community.

CHAPTER 5 ~ INTELLECTUAL MATURITY

MY INTELLECTUAL GOAL

MONTH _____

Sunday	Monday	Tuesday	Wednesday	Thursday	Friday	Saturday

I will try to _____
_____
_____
at least _____ times a week. If I am successful for _____ weeks in a row, I will feel _____.

If you don't achieve your goal, no worries. Just try again, or "tweak" your goal to make it more achievable.

CHAPTER 6

ETHICAL MATURITY

About Ethical Maturity

"Ethics" means understanding and being able to distinguish between right and wrong. Sometimes people who have good ethics are referred to as having good morals or values.

Only you can decide how you want to behave towards others. Some people refer to the "Golden Rule" as their ethical code: *Treat others the way you would like to be treated.*

When trying to mature into a healthy happy individual, taking care of your ethical health is very important. You will feel good about yourself if you are being a good person to those around you. This chapter will explore ways you can help develop and know yourself ethically.

CHAPTER 6 ~ ETHICAL MATURITY

VOLUNTEERING TO HELP OTHERS

Developing your ethical maturity is all about becoming the best person you can be. It's important to learn to love yourself first, but it's also important to reach out to those around you. Volunteering can help you feel good about yourself, and help give your life more meaning and depth. No one can take away the memories you will always have from giving your time and effort to others. Which of the following volunteer ideas sound interesting to you? Go to the Internet for contact information.

American Red Cross—Volunteer to help in their office, or try to raise money for disaster relief. Call your local Chapter to see what needs they might have.

_____Not for me. _____I looked into it.

Contact information: _____.

Church—Most churches have youth programs, and those organizations often do community service as one of their activities.

_____Not for me. _____I looked into it.

Contact information: _____.

Boy Scouts or Girl Scouts of America—These organizations help young people develop themselves in many of the areas of maturity, and most clubs volunteer for some cause. Call your local chapter.

_____Not for me. _____ I looked into it.

Contact information: _____

_____.

Hospitals—Most hospitals encourage young people to volunteer to help deliver items to the patients, and perform other tasks that help keep the patients happy.

_____Not for me. _____I looked into it.

Contact information: _____

_____.

MORE VOLUNTEERING IDEAS

Summer Camps—School districts and city parks programs usually offer summer safety camps and/or sports camps for the younger children. You could see if they need volunteers to lead a small group of campers. Other organizations that might need young people to volunteer in their camps are: Easter Seals, the Autism Society of America, Boys and Girls Club, and the YMCA.

_____Not for me. _____I looked into it.

Contact information: _____

Humane Society—Contact your local humane society to see if they need help with feeding, exercising, and/or the general care of the animals and their environments.

_____Not for me. _____I looked into it.

Contact information: _____

Museums—Is there a children's museum in your area? Perhaps you could see if they need some help.

_____Not for me. _____I looked into it.

Contact information: _____

Library—Maybe your local library could use some help shelving books, or help with some other tasks.

_____Not for me. _____I looked into it.

Contact information: _____

Special Olympics—Check out their website to see if they could use your help.

_____Not for me. _____I looked into it.

Contact information: _____

CHAPTER 6 ~ ETHICAL MATURITY

EVEN MORE VOLUNTEERING IDEAS!

Local Food Banks—Contact your local county food bank to see if you are needed in the warehouse, to sort or stack food.

_____Not for me. _____I looked into it.

Contact information: _____

Salvation Army, and other local organizations that reach out to those in need. Perhaps you could help serve food at a soup kitchen, or help in a thrift store that is sponsored by a non-profit organization.

_____Not for me. _____I looked into it.

Contact information: _____

Local retirement homes, nursing homes, or senior centers—The directors of these organizations are often looking for young people to sit and visit with their clients, especially the ones who do not have family living in the area. Maybe you could play an instrument for the clients, or bring a loving pet to share.

_____Not for me. _____I looked into it.

Contact information: _____

Relatives who might need help—If you have elderly relatives, or perhaps a relative with small children, and they live nearby, maybe you could volunteer to help them in some way.

_____Not for me. _____I looked into it.

Contact information: _____

Neighbors who might need help---Do you have elderly or disabled neighbors who could use your help with carrying groceries? Could you do yard work for someone? Are there people with small children that you could help entertain on a nice day?

_____Not for me. _____I looked into it.

Contact information: _____

Other ideas:

CHAPTER 6 ~ ETHICAL MATURITY

MY OPINIONS!

It shows that you have ethical maturity if you think and talk about how you feel about important issues. It is also important to talk to the adults in your life about how they hope you will approach some of these issues. React to the following statements, and give your reasoning for each answer. Come up with some statements of your own for the extra rows.

Statement	Strongly Agree	Agree	I'm in the Middle	Disagree	Strongly Disagree	Why I feel this way
Kids need chores.						
Everyone should volunteer.						
People should date for at least two years before deciding to marry.						
Kids should be paid for grades.						

CHAPTER 6 ~ ETHICAL MATURITY

WHAT ARE MY VALUES?

How do I want to live my life?
What behaviors should I choose that would make me safe, and proud of myself?

This is how I'd like to be treated by my family members:

Here are some ways I interact respectfully with my family members:

Here are some words that I would like my friends to use when they describe me and my behavior:

Here are some ideas for how I could probably improve my behavior so that people will appreciate and respect me more:

Here are some ways I can stick up for myself if someone tries to get me to do something I really don't want to do*:

---

*See Appendix, page 178, for *8 Ways to Say 'No' to Peer Pressure.*

THINKING AHEAD ABOUT CONSEQUENCES

This is a little exercise in "What if…?" Sometimes it's a good idea to think about the possible consequences of a situation before it ever comes up. Hopefully these situations won't come up, but it might solidify your values even more to think ahead of time about the consequences of certain behaviors, and how you want to deal with tough situations. For more help, see the section on *Refusal Skills*, pp. 102-103.

- What could happen if I skipped school and got caught?

- What could happen to my relationship with my parent(s) or guardian(s) if they found out I was not being honest with them?

- What could happen if I tried smoking?

- What would my life be like if I was addicted to smoking?

- What could happen if I tried drinking alcohol before I turn 21?

- How would my parent(s) or guardian(s) react if they caught me smoking or drinking?

- How would my life change if I was to become a teen parent?

CHAPTER 6 ~ ETHICAL MATURITY

EMPATHY:

MENTALLY IDENTIFYING WITH THE EXPERIENCES SOMEONE ELSE IS GOING THROUGH.

One sign of becoming *ethically mature* is when you have developed a sense of empathy for others. Read through the definition above. When you have empathy for someone, it means that you try to imagine what it might be like to go through what that person is experiencing.

Have you heard the phrase, "I wonder what it would be like to walk in his shoes"? If you really care to know what someone is going through, then you are developing empathy for that person. Fill in the following statements.

THIS IS WHAT IT MUST BE LIKE FOR SOMEONE WHO...

...is mentally handicapped:

...has only one arm:

...stutters when talking:

...is obese:

...lives in a foster home:

...is blind:

...is homeless:

MORE PRACTICE WITH EMPATHY

Continue to fill in these statements, trying to imagine what it would be like to be the person in each circumstance.

THIS IS WHAT IT MUST BE LIKE FOR SOMEONE WHO...

...is always being made fun of:

...is never hugged or told he or she is loved:

...is terminally ill:

...is deaf, or hard of hearing:

...is in a wheelchair:

...is of a different culture or religion:

...has a hard time learning:

...is very old:

...is afraid to leave his or her house:

EMPATHY CHALLENGES!

If you really want to know what it's like to be in someone's shoes, and challenge your ability to empathize with people, give one or more of the following challenges a try. Write about your experiences.

1. Borrow someone's wheelchair. Use it to get around and do what you need to do, for at least 2 hours.

2. Use only your non-dominant hand to make a peanut butter and jelly sandwich.

3. Wear a blindfold, and have someone use verbal instructions to tell you how to get from one place to another.

4. Sit at a table in the lunchroom, where you do not know anyone else who is sitting there.

5. Make arrangements to visit elderly people at a nearby nursing home. It would probably be best to have an adult accompany you.

6. Ask if you and a parent or guardian can help serve food at the local soup kitchen for the homeless.

7. Call the children's hospital and see if there is a patient you can visit and become friends with. Again, have an adult help you with this.

8. Think of your own empathy challenge:

WHAT WOULD I LIKE MY "EPITAPH" TO SAY?

When a person passes away, sometimes an epitaph is written on the tombstone. An epitaph is a brief poem or short statement about how that person chose to live his or her life, or about how they would like to be remembered. Usually a loved one writes the epitaph, but not always. Some people write their own epitaphs, before they pass away.

What would you like to have said about how you lived your life? Fill in the spaces on the tombstone, by writing your own epitaph. How would you like to be remembered?

WHEN WAS THE LAST TIME YOU DID A...
RAK?

(RANDOM ACT OF KINDNESS)

It feels good to do random acts of kindness for other people (and animals). One of the definitions in the dictionary for the word 'random' is purposeless. Have you ever performed a kind act for someone without having a purpose for doing it, other than to please that person? This means you did not expect or accept a reward.

Try doing something for someone without having a self-serving purpose in mind. Here are some examples: Clean the house without being asked; hold the door open for all of the other students; wash the car as a surprise; walk the dog without being told to do so; help a teacher or a new student.

Try coming up with some ideas of your own:

* _____

* _____

* _____

* _____

* _____

* _____

* _____

* _____

* _____

* _____

Now, on the next page, keep a log of your Acts of Kindness.

MY 'RAK' LOG*

On _____(date), I did this Act of Kindness: _____
_____.

This is how the person (or people) reacted: _____.

I felt _____ inside.

****

On _____(date), I did this Act of Kindness: _____
_____.

This is how the person (or people) reacted: _____.

I felt _____ inside.

****

On _____(date), I did this Act of Kindness: _____
_____.

This is how the person (or people) reacted: _____.

I felt _____ inside.

****

*A RAK is a Random Act of Kindness.

CHAPTER 6 ~ ETHICAL MATURITY

WHO ARE MY ROLE MODELS?

A role model is someone you look up to, someone you would like to emulate or imitate someday. Think about all of the adults in your life. Here are some of the possibilities: parents, guardians aunts, uncles, grandparents, older siblings and cousins, neighbors, teachers, coaches, church leaders, etc. Which of those adults display some of the qualities and values you would like to have someday? As you think about who your role models are, answer the questions below:

_____ is a role model for me. I especially like these qualities that I see in him or her:

_____

_____.

_____ is a role model for me. I especially like these qualities that I see in him or her:

_____

_____.

_____ is a role model for me. I especially like these qualities that I see in him or her:

_____

_____.

Is there someone younger than you who you hope to be a role model for someday? If so, who would that be? _____.

INSPIRATIONAL THOUGHTS FOR ETHICAL MATURITY

Now that you have experienced the chapter and filled in the pages on ethical maturity, look over the quotes below, highlighting and/or writing your reactions to the ones that inspire you the most. Authors names are listed when known.

- Everyone has some kind of prejudice, don't let yours control you.

- Be careful of what you allow to happen to yourself.

- Know when you've gone too far.

- Before you complain about your neighbor, clean up your own act.

- Help others. You'll feel better about yourself.

- Make a choice so no one will choose FOR you.

- Ask for nothing in return when giving gifts.

- You shouldn't give advice you don't follow. —Patricia C. Wrede

- No act of kindness, no matter how small, is ever wasted. —Aesop

- If you've given your personal power away, take it back.

- Respect others if you want to be respected. —Philippine proverb

- It is not how much we do, but how much love we put into the doing. —Mother Teresa

- You're not a failure if you fail. But, you're a failure if you blame someone else.— Edgar Burrow

- In seeking happiness for others, you find it for yourself.

- What we have done for ourselves alone dies with us; what we have done for others and the world remains, and is immortal.—Albert Pike

MORE INSPIRATIONAL THOUGHTS FOR ETHICAL MATURITY

Use the rest of this page to write other thoughts or quotes relating to your ethical health, that you make up or discover throughout your life.

- Liars are not believed even when they tell the truth. —Aesop

- You never really understand a person until you consider things from his point of view… until you climb into his skin and walk around in it. — Harper Lee

- Be kind, for everyone you meet is fighting a hard battle. —Plato

-
-
-
-
-
-
-
-

ETHICAL GOALS

This is an area you might already be working on. You are at that point in your life where you are probably trying to decide what type of person you want to become, perhaps through discussions with a parent or guardian, friends, and other important people in your life. Some ideas for goals in this area are listed below. Give them some thought, but then come up with just what it is that can help you mature ethically in your own little world, as well as in the big world we all live in. You might want to ask one of your adult role models to help you come up with this goal.

- Think of an act of kindness that you can do for someone who really could use the favor. Give it a try, take no reward, and see how good it feels.

- Go over the list of volunteer ideas on pages 147-149 and see if you are willing to look into a few of them. Find the phone numbers, make the calls, and find one that fits your personality and interests. Try it for at least one month.

- Give yourself an empathy challenge. Try living in someone else's shoes for a day. Could you not talk for a day? Use only one arm? Be blind?

- Make an opinion survey like the one on page 150, and ask 10 people their opinions.

- Have a conversation with your parent, guardian or grandparent about the values they hope for you to live by in your life.

- Use the calendar on the next page to mark off every day you go through where you only say kind words to the people you interact with.

- Ask your family if they'd like to help you donate services, food, or clothing to a specific charity or cause.

- Write a letter to an adult role model sharing why you love and appreciate them.

- Write a letter to yourself, about what kind of an individual you hope to become. Seal the letter and put it somewhere for safe keeping. Make a plan to open and read it on your 18th birthday.

CHAPTER 6 ~ ETHICAL MATURITY

MY ETHICAL GOAL

MONTH _____

Sunday	Monday	Tuesday	Wednesday	Thursday	Friday	Saturday

I will try to _____

_____ at least _____ times a week. If I am successful for _____ weeks in a row, I will feel _____.

If you don't achieve your goal, no worries. Just try again, or "tweak" your goal to make it more achievable.

APPENDIX

FUN THINGS TO DO & GOOD THINGS TO KNOW

BIRTH SIGNS

(Also known as Zodiac or Sun Signs)

Birth signs have to do with the position of the sun on the date you were born, and how that can affect your behavior and personality. You may have seen Horoscopes in the paper before. They are predictions for the future, (usually for that day), according to each birth sign. It's fun to learn about your birth sign, and read your horoscopes, but only you can determine what you're really going to be like, since you control your own behavior.

BIRTH DATE	BIRTH SIGN	SYMBOL
January 20—February 18	Aquarius	Waterbearer
February 19—March 20	Pisces	Fish
March 21—April 19	Aries	Ram
April 20—May 20	Taurus	Bull
May 21—June 20	Gemini	Twins
June 21—July 22	Cancer	Crab
July 23—August 22	Leo	Lion
August 23—September 22	Virgo	Virgin
September 23—October 22	Libra	Scales
October 23—November 21	Scorpio	Scorpion
November 22—December 21	Sagittarius	Archer
December 22—January 19	Capricorn	Sea Goat

FUN AND INTERESTING DAYS TO CELEBRATE EACH YEAR

Here is a list of only some of the fun and interesting days you could celebrate or learn about during the year. This is only part of the list that the author found at: **http://www.brownielocks.com.**

JANUARY

2-Happy Mew Year for Cats Day
3– J.R.R. Tolkien Day and National Chocolate Covered Cherry Day
4-Trivia Day and World Braille Day
8-Bubble Bath Day and Show and Tell Day at Work
10-National Cut Your Energy Costs Day
13-Rubber Duckie Day
14-Dress Up Your Pet Day and Organize Your Home Day
15 Humanitarian Day
16-Appreciate A Dragon Day
18-Pooh (Winnie The) Day and Thesaurus Day
21-National Hugging Day
23-National Handwriting Day and National Pie Day
24-Belly Laugh Day and National Compliment Day
27-Holocaust Memorial Day
29-Curmudgeons Day
30-Inane Answering Message Day

FEBRUARY

1-Decoration With Candy Day
2-Groundhog Day
4-World Cancer Day
5-World Nutella Day
7-Wear Red Day
9-Read in the Bathtub Day
11-National Shut-in Visitation Day
13-Get a Different Name Day
20—Love Your Pet Day

APPENDIX ~ THINGS TO DO & KNOW

MARCH
2-Dr. Seuss Day
6-Oreo Cookie Day
10-International Day of Awesomeness
17- St. Patrick's Day
18-Forgive Mom and Dad Day
25-Vaffeldagen (Waffle) Day
26-Make Up Your Own Holiday Day

APRIL
2-World Autism Day
10-National Sibling Day
12-D.E.A.R. Day-Drop Everything and Read Day
18-National Wear Your Pajamas to Work Day
23-Talk Like Shakespeare Day
27-Morse Code Day
30-Bugs Bunny Day

MAY
1-Mother Goose Day
3-National Two Different Colored Shoes Day
14-National Chicken Dance Day
18-Visit Your Relatives Day
21-National Endangered Species Day
23-National Toffee Day
31-Hug Your Cat Day

JUNE
1-Say Something Nice Day and Superman Day
6-Drive-in Movie Day
7-National Yo-Yo Day
12-National Peanut Butter Cookie Day
14-Family History Day
19-Garfield the Cat Day
23-Let It Go Day
27-PTSD Awareness Day

JULY
3-Compliment Your Mirror Day
7-Father-Daughter Take a Walk Together Day
10-Teddy Bear's Picnic Day
15-Gummi Worm Day
17-Yellow Pig Day
20-National Lollipop Day
27-Walk on Stilts Day

AUGUST
3-Watermelon Day
8-Happiness Happens Day
10-S'mores Day
13-International Left Hander's Day
15-National Relaxation Day
18-Bad Poetry Day
21-Senior Citizen's Day
25-National Second-Hand Wardrobe Day

SEPTEMBER
5-International Day of Charity
9-Wonderful Weirdoes Day
10-Swap Ideas Day
16-Stepfamily Day
19-Talk Like a Pirate Day
22-Dear Diary Day
25-National One-Hit Wonder Day
27-Ancestor Appreciation Day
28-National Good Neighbor Day

OCTOBER
1-International Music Day
4-National Taco Day
5-World Teachers Day
10-World Mental Health Day
13-National Chess Day
15-National Cake Decorating Day and National Grouch Day
22-National Nut Day
31-Halloween and National Knock Knock Joke Day

NOVEMBER
1-Extra Mile Day
2-Plan Your Epitaph Day
10-National Tongue Twister Day and Sesame Street Day
14-National Pickle Day
18-Mickey Mouse Day
20-Universal Children's Day
25-International Hat Day

DECEMBER
4-National Cookie Day
7-National Pearl Harbor Remembrance Day
10-Nobel Prize Day
16-National Chocolate Covered Anything Day
21-Crossword Puzzle Day
26-National Thank You Card Day

THINGS TO DO WHEN YOU'RE BORED AT HOME:

1. Fold tin foil into fun shapes.
2. Draw a picture or make a maze.
3. Make a healthy snack (from the list of suggestions on pages 74-75!).
4. Read your old children's books.
5. Make something out of duct tape.
6. Make a photo album or scrap book.
7. Find fabric scraps and create a piece of clothing, or add to an existing piece.
8. Play with a slinky.
9. Get out a jigsaw puzzle.
10. Read food labels.
11. Listen to music.
12. Write a poem or song.
13. Make a card for someone.
14. Make a first aid kit for the family.
15. Make a fort.
16. Clean the house as a surprise.
17. Ask someone to play a board game with you.
18. Try a crossword puzzle, a Sudoku, or a word search.
19. Make a list of emergency phone #'s to put next to the phone and/or into your phone contacts. (pg. 65).
20. Practice your multiplication tables by making flashcards.
21. Paint faces on peanuts.
22. Learn something new out of an encyclopedia, a thesaurus, or a dictionary.
23. Build something with your LEGO® or block collection.
24. Play solitaire, or ask someone to play a card game with you.
25. Make a goal, and a chart to go with it.
26. Draw anything that comes to mind, and then write a story about it.
27. Try a new recipe.
28. Clean your room and rearrange the furniture in it.
29. Learn how to play chess.
30. Invent something, maybe using reusable items.
31. Walk to your old elementary school and play on the playground equipment.
32. Walk the dog, if you have one. Or, offer to walk a friend's or neighbor's dog.
33. Make food for the squirrels or birds.
34. Play NERF® basketball, or create your own basket and ball.
35. Alphabetize something. Your CD's? The spices in the cupboard?
36. Clean out your closet and drawers.
37. Call the city bus company and find out schedules for your neighborhood, and the places where you'd like to go.
38. Research a topic that interests you.
39. Write out a scavenger hunt for a family member or a friend.

MORE THINGS TO DO WHEN BORED!

40. Go for a walk or a jog.
41. Take a bubble bath.
42. Take photos.
43. Dance.
44. Lift weights. If you don't have any, try heavy books, or cans of food.
45. Ride your bike.
46. Walk to the store and take back the bottles and cans.
47. Make a piggy bank.
48. Make a calendar. Put a different photo on each month.
49. Do your homework, or some extra credit.
50. Call a radio station and request a song.
51. Study the clouds.
52. Wash the car for a nice surprise.
53. Pick flowers and put them in a vase.
54. Practice saying the alphabet backwards.
55. Make a collage of pictures of fruits and vegetables to put on the refrigerator door.
56. Blow bubbles.
57. Call a friend or relative. How about a grandparent?
58. Bird watch.
59. Make a collage for the wall, your binder, or the cover of a journal.
60. Make a new recorded message on the phone.
61. Start to learn a foreign language. How about sign language?
62. Visit an elderly neighbor and ask if you can wash their car, or help in some other way.
63. Try to start a collection of something.
64. Make a movie.
65. Organize something. How about the junk drawer?
66. Make a toy for your pet, or your friend's pet.
67. Plan a party.
68. Jump rope.
69. Play hide and seek with someone.
70. Practice cursive, or fancy printing.
71. Learn about a musical instrument.
72. Start a journal. Don't forget to decorate the cover.
73. Draw a cartoon.
74. Make a cookbook of your family's favorite recipes.
75. Try a makeover or a new hairstyle.
76. Work on your next Halloween costume.
77. Make play dough (see page 175).
78. Decorate your room with Christmas lights.
79. Play with a yo-yo.
80. Change your sheets.
81. Write compliments to your family members on sticky notes and put them on mirrors throughout the house.
82. Write your life story.

EVEN MORE THINGS TO DO WHEN BORED!

83. Sit in a tree and read or write.
84. Make juice popsicles or ice cubes.
85. Practice shuffling cards, making a house of cards, or a card trick.
86. Write a letter.
87. Make a flyer about your job skills and take it around the neighborhood.
88. Fix something. Or, take apart something and see how it works.
89. Mend a piece of clothing.
90. Start a bug collection.
91. Create a vegetable or herb garden.
92. Play Jacks.
93. Make or design a tree fort.
94. Ask a friend to throw or kick around a ball with you.
95. Play "school" with a sibling or a neighborhood child.
96. Read the Drivers Manual.
97. Look at maps.
98. Make a birdhouse.
99. Organize a neighborhood kid parade.
100. Make a model of something with toothpicks and glue.
101. Find the candles and make sure the flashlights work, to prepare the family for an emergency.
102. Make a list of things to do.
103. Sharpen all of the pencils and organize a study area.
104. Finger paint.
105. Make placemats or place cards for the family.
106. Read a book, a magazine, or look at the newspaper.
107. Look at your parent's or guardian's old high school yearbook.
108. Stretch.
109. Look up world records.
110. Practice relaxation techniques.
111. Clean the fridge.
112. Look around the garage or your room for something to play with.
113. Try juggling three items that are similar in size and shape.
114. Vacuum.
115. Make paper airplanes.
116. Fill in some of the pages in this book.
117. Make a Lemonade Stand.
118. Look into volunteer opportunities.
119. Make wrapping paper using paper bags or plain paper.
120. Organize a family activity or picnic.
121. Play Hacky Sack.
122. Kick a ball or hit a tennis ball with a racket against a wall.
123. Plan out an act of kindness you can surprise someone with.
124. Try some of the physical challenges that are listed in the physical chapter, pages 82-84.
125. Make a sign for your bedroom door.

PARTY THEME IDEAS

Hollywood/Movies

Sports in general or a specific sport

Decades: 50's, 60's, 70's, 80's, etc.

Beach/Luau/Pool

Fiesta

Pirate

Oriental

Science Fiction

Superhero

Any of the holidays

Any of the seasons

A major event, such as a graduation or anniversary

Book Characters

Zoo Animals/Dinosaurs

EASY TO MAKE OR FIND: STRESS RELIEVERS

- Look up a recipe for homemade bath salts.

- Play with clay, or play dough, (recipe on the next page).

- Make a "rice sock" and put it in the microwave for a few seconds, then place it on your neck. It just takes a sock and some rice! Be careful not to get it too hot.

- Hammer some nails on a piece of wood.

- Go for a brisk walk or a jog.

- Write down what is making you angry and then tear it up.

- Use a pillow as a punching bag.

- Go somewhere where you are all alone and scream. Inside a car? At the ocean?

- Dance to music, all by yourself in your room.

- Draw or paint, even finger painting will work.

- Try one of the relaxation techniques in this book.

- Listen to relaxing music or nature sounds.

- Make a little sand castle with wet sand, or play with a tray of dry sand.

Can you think of any more?

-

-

PLAY DOUGH RECIPE*

- 2 Tbsp. alum
- 2 cups flour
- 1 cup salt
- 1 cup water
- 2 Tbsp. oil
- A few drops of your choice of food coloring

Mix together the first three (dry) ingredients. Stir the food coloring and the oil together. Pour the liquid ingredients into the dry ingredients carefully while you mix them together. Knead. Store in plastic containers in the refrigerator. Have fun!

*This recipe is one of many play dough recipes that can be found at

www.PlayDoughRecipe.com

SKILLS YOU CAN TEACH YOURSELF

WITH THE AID OF A BOOK OR YouTube VIDEO

- Serve or spike a volleyball.
- Speak another language.
- Make paper airplanes.
- All types of dance moves.
- Get organized.
- Solve a Rubik's Cube.
- Wood carving or woodworking.
- Play a keyboard or guitar.
- Put spin on a tennis or ping pong ball.
- Magic tricks.
- Braid hair and create other hairstyles.
- Take notes or study for a test.
- Throw a baseball or softball.
- Take a good photograph.
- Make slime.
- Swing a bat.
- Ride a unicycle.
- Cook just about anything.
- Plant a garden.

APPENDIX ~ THINGS TO DO & KNOW

WHAT DOES A SERVING LOOK LIKE?

ITEM TO MEASURE:	MEASUREMENT:
Beef, Pork or Chicken	The palm of your hand, or a deck of cards
Fish	A checkbook
Nuts	Small handful
Peanut Butter	Golf Ball
Cheese	One package string cheese or 4 dice
Salad or Cereal	Both servings would fit in cupped hands
Potato or Fresh Fruit	Both would be the size of a small fist
Pancake or Waffle	A compact disc
Pasta	Tennis ball, or rounded handful
A teaspoon of anything	The top joint on an average thumb
A Tablespoon of anything	An average-sized thumb

8 WAYS TO SAY "NO" TO PEER PRESSURE*

When someone, (or a group of friends), tries to get to you do something you don't want to do, it is important that you speak clearly and firmly, and have good posture to show that you mean what you say. You might want to question whether you have selected friends that have the same goals and morals as you do, if this continues to be a problem.

Here are some suggestions for how you can respond:

1. Say "No" clearly, or perhaps it's best to say, "No way. Why would I want to do that?"

2. State the facts. Tell the person why it wouldn't be a good idea, and name the unhealthy consequences.

3. Change the subject, or suggest a fun alternative activity you could do together.

4. If you've already said "No", and someone continues to pressure you, reverse the pressure back to him. Say, "Why do you continue to pressure me after I've already told you I don't want to do it?"

5. Ignore the request and just walk away.

6. If you know someone is going to ask you to do something you don't want to do, steer clear of the person. Don't be alone with him or her.

7. Use humor, or say, "You're kidding, right?"

8. Make up an excuse. Say that you have to do something else at that time. After all, not getting in trouble is doing something!

*You could also practice the five-step refusal skills method described on pp. 102-103.

THINGS TO THINK ABOUT WHEN SETTING GOALS

- The first two letters of goal are GO!

- Shared goals build unity.

- If at first you didn't succeed, you're normal.

- You have to give up the way you are to have it the way you want.

- You are the only one who can stop You from doing something permanently.

- Don't continue to do the same things if you don't like what you're getting out of them.

- You'll never know what you can't do if you don't try.

- Begin with the first step.

- The only thing that prevents you from reaching your goals is you.

- Go confidently in the direction of your dreams. Live the life you have imagined.—Henry David Thoreau

- The greatest freedom you have is the freedom to discipline yourself.—Bernard Baruch

THINGS TO THINK ABOUT WHEN DEALING WITH LOSS

- Don't hurt others because you've been hurt.
- You can't solve your problems by escaping from them.
- Realize when you are hurting.
- Don't let yesterday rule today.
- Take the first step towards forgiveness.
- Benefits come from each failure or disappointment, if you look hard enough.
- Walls that you've built within are not sturdy enough to keep you strong.
- Healing brings forgiveness.
- Recover for yourself first.
- Let go of pain.
- Don't wallow in self-pity.
- Forgiveness replaces bitterness.
- Layers of resentment bury joy.
- Give the gift of forgiveness.
- Release feelings in a healthy way.
- The future is never as dark as the past.
- Life can be changed, by changing your thinking.
- Everyone thinks their load is heavier.
- Tie a knot and hang on when you feel that you are at the end of your rope.
- If you want a rainbow, you have to get through the rain.

SIGNS AND SYMPTOMS THAT YOU OR A FRIEND MIGHT HAVE AN EATING DISORDER

There are several types of eating disorders. This is a very serious subject. An adult that is related to the individual, or working with the individual closely, such as a parent or guardian, or a school counselor, should be consulted, if you suspect that you, or someone close to you has an eating disorder.

Someone who is suffering from an eating disorder does not necessarily always appear to be underweight, or average weight, or overweight. And, of course many times the individual is in denial about his or her disease. This makes it even more difficult to follow your instincts if you are concerned about yourself or a friend.

Below are only some of the signs that someone might have an eating disorder.
(Source: **www.something-fishy.org/isf/signssymptoms.php**)

- Wearing the type of clothing that would hide a body shape, like loose or baggy clothes.
- Being obsessed with how much you weigh, or how big you think you are.
- Obsessing over how much fat and how many calories are in the food you eat.
- Continually exercising.
- Makes several trips to the bathroom after eating, and sometimes running water while in the bathroom, to hide any hint that you might be vomiting.
- Noticeably starving or restricting yourself from food.
- Using diet pills or laxatives.
- Not wanting to eat around other people. Isolating yourself in general.
- Hiding food in an effort not to eat it, or to eat it later.
- Constantly keeping a journal of calories eaten, exercise, etc.
- Physical problems such as: hair loss; pale skin; feeling dizzy; headaches; sore throat; menstrual period stopping; feeling cold; bloodshot eyes; fatigue; high or low blood pressure; and poor sleeping habits.
- Showing a strong need for approval. Making comments about how fat or stupid you are.
- Always trying a new type of diet.
- Feeling that life would be so much better if you lost weight.
- Mood swings or depression.

National Eating Disorder Association Helpline:
1-800-931-2237

APPENDIX ~ THINGS TO DO & KNOW

HELPLINES

Poison Control 1-800-222-1222

Alcohol and Drug Helpline 1-800-784-6776

Al-Anon / Alateen 1-888-425-2666

National AIDS Hotline 1-800-232-4636

Sexually Transmitted Disease Hotline 1-800-232-4636

Gay and Lesbian National Hotline 1-888-843-4564

National Mental Health Hotline 1-800-273-TALK (8255)

Youth Suicide Prevention 1-800-784-2433

Child Help USA (Abuse Hotline) 1-800-4-A-CHILD

National Eating Disorder Association Helpline
1-800-931-2237

APPENDIX ~ THINGS TO DO & KNOW

DECISION-MAKING HELP
HALTS!

HALTS! is an acronym that will help you during times of stress. An acronym is when a word or an abbreviation is formed from the first initials of a phrase or group of words. In this case, HALTS is the perfect acronym to think of in times of stress, because if you feel Hungry, Angry, Lonely, Tired or Sick, you really should *Halt*, or stop, and take a break before reacting to stress, or making a difficult decision. Those times when you aren't at your best are times when you might regret any big decision you make, any words that come out of your mouth, or any physical action you might display.

Can you remember a time when you perhaps skipped a meal, or you weren't eating properly, and you became rather *testy*, or cranky? There's a word for that. You were feeling *hypoglycemic*. That means you had low blood sugar, or glucose, which is an energy source. If you don't take care of it by having a healthy snack, then you might unintentionally lash out at someone. Remember, the H in HALTS stands for **Hungry**.

Something that was discussed earlier in the book, (on page 52), was a defense mechanism we sometimes use when we're angry. It's called displacement. When you use displacement, you project your anger onto someone or something. If you find yourself wanting to hit someone or something, stop and recognize your feeling for what it is—anger. Give yourself a timeout, time to breathe and think, before you do or say something you might regret later. Remember, the A in HALTS is for **Anger**.

We all get Lonely from time to time. Loneliness is part of life. We all need to know how to handle being alone in a positive way, by doing things like reading, writing, or perhaps drawing. Try not to make a decision if you are feeling too lonely. Put the decision off for awhile, and find a creative outlet. Remember, the L in HALTS is for **Lonely**.

Especially during the school year, with the new sleep, homework and activity schedules, we can get tired very easily. If you find that you are making poor decisions, ask yourself if the reason you are not thinking correctly is because maybe you're too tired. If so, stop, take a rest break, maybe even try listening to some calming sounds or music, and then approach the problem with a refreshed mind. Remember, the T in HALTS is for **Tired**.

And finally, the S in HALTS, which stands for **Sick**. Your body systems, (which includes all of your cells, tissues and organs) are interrelated. If you're sick, your immune system isn't working at 100%. That means your nervous system (the one that contains the brain) will also be affected. Give yourself time to mend before you make a big decision. Usually the best decisions are made when we give ourselves time to think through the pros, the cons, and the possible repercussions from each choice.

HALTS—Hungry, Angry, Lonely, Tired, Sick.

TYPES OF COLLEGE DEGREES

Have you ever wondered what it means when someone says they have a Bachelor's Degree? Does that mean that the person studied about bachelors? It can be very confusing when people talk about the different types of college degrees. Here is some basic information that might help you understand the different types of degrees. There are other courses of study besides the ones listed here. For example, someone could go to a college that specifically helps people become licensed or certified in certain skills. Examples would be: cosmetology, medical assisting, medical transcription, and culinary arts. So, if we look only at college degrees, here are the basics, listed in the order of how much education is required, going from least to most.

ASSOCIATE'S DEGREE

*This is basically a two year program, although some people take longer to complete the coursework.

*Sometimes this represents the first two years of a four year program that will lead to a Bachelor's Degree, and the credits need to be transferred to a four year school.

*There are different types of Associate's Degrees, depending on the types of classes taken. An AA is an Associate of Arts degree. An AS is an Associate of Science degree. There are also AAS and AFA degrees: Associate of Applied Sciences and Associate of Fine Arts.

BACHELOR'S DEGREE

*This represents the completion of a four year program. The student usually *majors* in a particular subject area. Sometimes a student will major in more than one area, or major in one subject area, and minor in another subject area. The program can take longer than, or even shorter than four years to complete, depending on how many classes are taken at one time; whether or not a class is retaken in order to earn a better grade; and whether or not the student attends summer terms.

*Similar to the Associate's Degree, there are different types of Bachelor's degrees: BA (Bachelor of Arts), and BS (Bachelor of Science) are the two main areas, but there are others.

*Within a four year college or university there are different *schools*, depending on the subject area a student is majoring in. Examples would be: The School of Journalism; The School of Business Administration; The School of Physical Education, and so on.

MASTER'S DEGREE

*This degree can be earned after someone earns a Bachelor's Degree. A master's degree, is also called a graduate degree. The program usually takes approximately two years to complete, and consists of coursework taken in a concentrated subject area. Some jobs require a master's degree. Plus, in some careers, the more education you have the more money you can earn.

*Similar to both the associate's and the bachelor's degrees, a master's degree can be an MS, an MA, or one of the other types of masters. Masters candidates often write a paper called a *thesis*.

DOCTORATE'S DEGREE

*This is the highest graduate degree one can earn. It is usually called a PhD, (doctor of philosophy), although there is also a JD, (doctor of jurisprudence), which is an advanced law degree. The program of studies can take 5-10 years to complete. Doctoral candidates write a long in-depth paper called a *dissertation*.

*A doctorate's degree is usually associated with scientists and professors.

BIBLIOGRAPHY

Armstrong, Thomas, PhD. *You're Smarter Than You Think. A Kid's Guide to Multiple Intelligences*. Minneapolis, MN: Free Spirit Publishing, Inc., 2003.

"Backpack Safety Quiz-How to Wear Your Backpack for a Healthy Back." *Pearson Chiropractic and Rehabilitation Center.* N.p., n.d. Web 4 Aug. 2011. http://www.pearsonchiropractic.com/resources/backpack-safety-quiz/.

Bennett, Elizabeth. *It's My Year Passbook.* New York, NY: Tangerine Press, 2009.

Biegal, Gina. *The Stress Reduction Workbook for Teens*. Oakland, CA: Instant Help Books, 2009.

"Bizarre Silly Crazy Goofy Dumb Daily Calendar." *Brownielocks and the 3 Bears.* n.p., 25 Jan.v2010. Web 3 Aug. 2011.

Borgenicht, David, Ben H. Winters and Robin Epstein. *The Worst Case Scenario Survival Handbook: Middle School.* San Francisco, CA: Quirk Productions, Inc., 2009.

Carlson, Richard. *Don't Sweat the Small Stuff for Teens-Journal.* New York, NY: Hyperion. 2002.

Choron, Sandra and Harry. *The Book of Lists for Teens*. New York, NY: Houghton Mifflin Company, 2002.

Covey, Sean. *The 7 Habits of Highly Effective Teens.* New York, NY: Fireside, Franklin Covey Company. 1998.

Engelmann, Jeanne. *Pass It On At School (Activity Handouts for Creating Caring Schools).* Minneapolis, MN: The Search Institute, 2003.

Erlbach, Arlene. *The Middle School Survival Guide.* New York, NY: Walker Publishing Co., 2003.

Fuller, Rose, and Andrew Asato. *I'm in Charge of the Facts.* Portland, OR: Northwest Family Services, n.g.

Graff, Cynthia Stamper and Jerry Holden. *Lean for Life, Phase One.* Torrence, CA: Griffin Publishing Group, 2001.

BIBLIOGRAPHY

Grothe, Rebecca. *More Building Assets Together.* Minneapolis, MN: Search Institute, 2002.

Graydon, Shari. *In Your Face.* Buffalo, NY: Annick Press Ltd., 2004.

Harrison, Henry H. *1001 Things Every Teen Should Know Before They Leave Home (Or Else They'll Come Back).* Nashville, TN: Thomas Nelson Publishers, 2007.

Kramer, Patricia. *Discovering the Real You.* New York, NY: The Rosen Publishing Group, Inc., 1991.

Lewis, Barbara. *What Do You Stand For? A Kid's Guide to Building Character.* Minneapolis, MN: Free Spirit Publishing, Inc., 1998.

"Louis Braille Biography." *Braille Bug Site.* American Federation for the Blind, 2010. Web. 3 Aug. 2011.

McGraw, Jay. *Life Strategies for Teens.* New York, NY: Fireside, 2000.

Mosatche, Harriet and Karen Unger. *Too Old For This! Too Young For That!—Your Survival Guide for the Middle-School Years.* Minneapolis, MN: Free Spirit Publishing, Inc., 2000.

Ogden, Cynthia, and Margaret Carroll. "NCHS Health E-Stat." *CDC-Center for Disease Control and Prevention.* N.p., 4 Apr. 2011. Web. 21 July 2011. http://www.cdc.gov/obesity/childhood/data.html.

Phillips, Karen. *It's All About Me! Personality Quizzes for You and Your Friends.* Palo Alto, CA: Klutz, 2006.

Phillips, Karen. *My All-Time Top 5—A Book of Lists for You and Your Friends.* Palo Alto, CA: Klutz, 2008.

"Posture Problems-Straight Talk About Slouching." *Mothernature.com* n.d. Web 4 Aug. 2011. http://www.mothernature.com/archive/centers/detail.cfm?id=378&term=Rash.

Prigg, Mark. *MailOnline-health.* N.d. Web 4 Aug. 2011. http://www.dailymail.co.uk/health/article-203388/Poor-posture-causing-kids-problems.html.

Rimm, Sylvia. *Rescuing the Emotional Lives of Overweight Children—What Our Kids Go Through and How We Can Help.* n.g.: Rodale, 2004.

Roehlkepartain, Jolene L. *Building Assets Together, 135 Group Activities for Helping Youth Succeed*. Minneapolis, MN: Search Institute, 1997.

Vandenburg, Mary Lou. *Coping With Being Shy*. New York, NY: The Rosen Publishing Group, Inc., 1993.

ABOUT THE AUTHOR

Mary Richards is a retired health and physical education teacher who is still involved in the classroom. She has always had a passion for wellness and a desire to motivate others, especially her students, towards self-improvement. The majority of Mary's career was spent in the middle-school classroom. In addition to being in the classroom, Mary has coached kids in sports and directed plays. During her career she launched dance teams, jump rope teams, weight-loss clubs, a drug-free club, a community health fair, a pet fair, and a self-esteem club, *Feeling Good*.

Born and raised in Oregon, Mary spent her early years in North Bend. She received her BS and MS degrees from the University of Oregon in Eugene. Her teaching career included assignments in Bandon, Coos Bay, Springfield, and Salem, Oregon; and Caracas, Venezuela. Wherever she has been, helping kids improve their self-esteem has been her number one priority. In 1988, when 6th grade was still part of the elementary school, Mary was named *Elementary Educator of the Year* for Salem-Keizer schools.

Mary enjoys spending time with family and friends, helping her sweetheart build a log cabin, playing the piano, singing karaoke, going to the gym, driving her 1968 VW bug, writing a wellness blog (The Fit Optimist), fishing, traveling (cruises), volunteering and playing table tennis. She has also amassed a pretty impressive Pez® collection. Mary can be reached at: **awesomeworkbook@gmail.com** .

ACKOWLEDGEMENTS

I have immense gratitude for all the family, friends, colleagues and students who believed in my project and have offered continuous support and encouragement along the way. A special shout-out goes to those of you who were willing to provide feedback on short notice.

To Emily Walbridge, of Creative Simplicity, I am thankful for your prompt and friendly editing services.

Additionally my heartfelt thanks to Suzanne Fyhrie Parrott, of First Steps Publishing, for her professionalism, guidance, and exceptional talent, enabling this project to finally come to fruition.

I would also like to thank Suzanne for discovering and hiring Carrie Brandon, artist extraordinaire.

Because of all of you, I feel truly blessed.